C000053474

IRONY AND IDENTITY
in Modern Irish Drama

ONDŘEJ PILNÝ

þ

Litteraria Pragensia
Prague 2006

Copyright © Ondřej Pilný, 2006

Published 2006 by Litteraria Pragensia
Faculty of Philosophy, Charles University
Náměstí Jana Palacha 2, 116 38 Prague 1
Czech Republic
www.litterariapragensia.com

All rights reserved. This book is copyright under international copyright conventions. Except for provisions made under "fair use," no part of this book may be reproduced, stored in a retrieval system, or transmitted in any form, electronic, mechanical, photocopying, recording or otherwise, without prior written permission from the copyright holders. Requests to publish work from this book should be directed to the publishers.

The publication of this book has been supported by research grant MSM0021620824 "Foundations of the Modern World as Reflected in Literature and Philosophy" awarded to the Faculty of Philosophy, Charles University, Prague, by the Czech Ministry of Education.

Cataloguing in Publication Data

    Irony and Identity in Modern Irish Drama, by Ondřej Pilný. — 1st ed.
    p. cm.
      ISBN 80-7308-126-1 (pb)
      1. Drama. 2. Irish Studies. 3. Post-Colonialism.
      I. Pilný, Ondřej. II. Title

Cover image: *Pietà / Il Commendatore* © Anna Chromy, 2000

Printed in the Czech Republic by PB Tisk
Typesetting & design by lazarus

Contents

Introduction 1

I. VISIONS
The Home of Ancient Idealism
W.B. Yeats and the Irish Dramatic Movement 11

Man is not Fashioned as are the Swine and Stars
J.M. Synge 36

II. REJECTIONS
Not a Theme for Poetry
Sean O'Casey and *The Silver Tassie* 71

Up the Living Departed!
Denis Johnston's *The Old Lady Says "No!"* 85

III. REVISIONS
Mythologies of Fantasy and Hope
Brian Friel and Field Day 105

Comedy of Terrors
Stewart Parker 135

Disconcert and Destabilise the Prisoner
Martin McDonagh 154

Bibliography 170
Index 182

Introduction

Collective identity has been a dominant theme throughout the history of modern Irish drama, from the time of the Irish Literary Theatre up until the current cultural changes resulting from the economic boom in the late 1990s. The initial effort to represent collective identity on the stage was inseparably bound with the Irish national revival, and as such has been analogous to many revivals of national cultures across Europe. The persistence with which the issue has been recurring in Irish theatre throughout the twentieth century, and especially its latter half, may be attributed chiefly to the conflict in (and over) Northern Ireland, while most recently—although arguably this stems from different motivations and objectives—also to the impact of globalisation on Ireland.

The aim of this book is to examine several important phases in the history of the staging of Ireland, focusing on significant transformations which have been apparent in the approach of playwrights and theatre groups to the issue. The establishment of an Irish national theatre under W.B. Yeats and Lady Gregory is discussed first, looking at the proclaimed aims of the "Irish Dramatic Movement," the actual work of what was later to become the National Theatre and its interaction with its audiences and its critics. This is followed by an exploration of how the Abbey Theatre had grown into a largely conservative force, opposing the experimentation and political challenges propounded by talented emergent playwrights such as Sean

O'Casey and Denis Johnston. The third part of this volume opens with an examination of the Field Day Theatre Company, a group enterprise which has been linked, particularly by its opponents, to the Revival due to its efforts at positing a revised version of Irish identity. The discussion of Field Day also reflects on the broad involvement of all its projects with culture in Ireland, North and South alike, and underscores some essential difficulties that have emerged concerning Field Day's post-colonial definition and its attempt to craft a non-hegemonic metanarrative of Irishness. Subsequently, the work of one of Ireland's most innovative yet relatively neglected playwrights, Stewart Parker, is analysed, focusing on the way in which his drama undermines any emphasis on the revision of metanarrative by constantly reformulating theatrical principles. Finally, the engagement of contemporary drama with collective identity is exemplified by the plays of Martin McDonagh, the self-styled *enfant terrible* of Irish drama. A critical look at his work serves as a coda of the argument, summing up the difficulties entailed in essentialist definitions of identity and highlighting the persistence of the discourse of Irishness in contemporary theatre, be it only as a momentous ambivalent legacy.

The method the present work uses to address the issue of collective identity is the identification of irony in the complex network of forces involved in defining national identity in Ireland through its theatre. Within this strategy, some degree of attention is paid to Socratic irony (the deliberate understatement of one's knowledge and abilities, or alternately "pretended simplicity"[1] used as a rhetorical tool in a dialectical quest for truth) and dramatic irony (a plot device which has the spectators know significantly more than the character they are watching, or which contrasts the character's understanding of his/her actions with what the play demonstrates about them); however, these types of irony are of secondary interest given the overall concerns of this book. The focus is predominantly on

---

[1] D.C. Muecke, *The Compass of Irony*, 2nd ed. (London: Methuen, 1980) 88.

irony in its Romantic form, that is, irony as a philosophical and aesthetic stance that serves to comment on the apparent incongruities and paradoxes of the world.

The concept of irony employed here thus builds in particular on the ideas of Friedrich Schlegel and Søren Kierkegaard—the fathers of Romantic irony—and how they have been interpreted and developed in the second half of the twentieth century by Douglas Muecke, Wayne Booth, Lilian Furst, Paul de Man, and ultimately Linda Hutcheon.[2] Hutcheon expands upon earlier concepts, and reflecting the approach of post-structuralist theory to language, she argues that irony is an event which "comes into being in the relations between meanings, but also between people and utterances and, sometimes, between intentions and interpretations."[3] Irony hence becomes a matter of communication, intertextual as well as, for instance, interpersonal or inter-institutional. Hutcheon moreover emphasises that it is the interpreter who ultimately attributes irony to a particular text or passage, while his/her interpretive activity takes place regardless of the ironist's intention; this is not to imply any salutary disregard for what may have been intended but rather to point out the difficulties in transmitting irony to the interpreter, including the fact that the attitudes of the two need not converge. The interpreter's attribution of irony involves not only the "making or inferring of meaning," but also expressing or implying a particular value judgement of both the said and the unsaid, which again may or may not be the same as the ironist's. In short, the identification of irony involves "both semantic and evaluative inferences."[4] As far as evaluation is concerned, the core of the matter is of course that

[2] For a detailed critical summary of their approaches, see Ondřej Pilný, "Concepts of Irony," *Acta Universitatis Carolinae—Philologica* 2, 2005/ Prague Studies in English XXIV (Prague: The Karolinum Press, 2006) 141-56. References to relevant sources on irony will be found in the bibliography to the present volume.

[3] Linda Hutcheon, *Irony's Edge. The Theory and Politics of Irony* (London: Routledge, 1994) 13.

[4] Hutcheon, *Irony's Edge*, 11.

any evaluation ultimately leads towards the Schlegelian ironising of its very grounds, or in other words, it queries the basis from which the values themselves arise.[5]

Each section in the present volume adopts a variation of the general approach which seemed best suited to its subject matter, in an attempt to foreground the multiplicity of fundamental issues inherent in the theatre of identity. The opening section which discusses the work and ideas of W.B. Yeats and J.M. Synge uses detailed theatre history in order to demonstrate an ironic tension between the explicit objectives of their Irish national theatre on the one hand and the actual theatrical practice on the other, particularly as regards the depiction of the Irish people in Synge's and Yeats's plays and its controversial political resonance. While the essential coherence of the metanarrative of the national theatre under the leadership of W.B. Yeats is foregrounded, attention is drawn to the numerous intricate shifts in public rhetoric, and also how a theatre project established in order to propound the ancient idealist nature of the Irish nation gradually began to devote a considerable amount of time to defending the freedom of speech in the face of collective hostility from the same nation. The ultimate focus, above all with the plays of Synge, is the imperative authenticity of representation, the primary requirement of a national theatre at the time of the Revival, and for that matter, at many other times. In addition to this, the chapter dedicated to J.M. Synge shows irony serving as a means of satire, not on the mores of the country people but rather a particular kind of urban nationalists. Despite the local satirical note, however, Synge is also seen as a Romantic and a humanist, striving to create a universally valid poetic—and moral—message.

---

5 This aspect of Romantic irony has been recently discussed, for instance, by Martin Procházka; see Martin Procházka, "Seasons in K.H. Mácha's *May* and Byron's Poetry: A Reading of Two Ironical Strategies," *Byron: A Poet for All Seasons*, ed. Marios Byron Raizis (Messolonghi: Messolonghi Byron Society, 2000) 209-19.

The discussion of the early years of the Irish national theatre is continued in the second part of this volume which pays attention to significant rejections by the Abbey Theatre directorate. Two challenging plays are studied in particular: Sean O'Casey's *The Silver Tassie* and Denis Johnston's *The Old Lady Says "No!"* Although principally very different, both dramas are joined in their critique of heroism, and even more importantly perhaps, in their innovative use of avant-garde and modernist techniques. Despite their focus on narratives of collective identity, neither of the plays was deemed suitable to be staged at the National Theatre. The analysis of their politics and aesthetic serves to underline the ingenious employment of irony in the context of non-naturalist revisioning of the dominant discourse of identity, together with further ironies concerning the conservatism and self-enclosed nature of the Abbey's practice at least from the 1920s onwards.

The subsequent examination of Field Day opens up several theoretical issues related to narratives of identity. Apart from sketching out the affinities between the nationalist and the post-colonial positions, the interpretation offered here centres around the employment of notions such as demythologisation and an ideal world consisting solely of micro-narratives adopted by Field Day from the work of Jean-François Lyotard. The utopian nature of Lyotard's vision, especially when applied to a highly politicised context defined to a large extent by the violent impasse in Northern Ireland in the 1980s, is shown to be more than evident. This is also documented by the thematic shift—viewed as ironical in the context of the Field Day project—which is apparent in Brian Friel's plays from that decade: Friel's initial focus on narrative gradually yields to one on communication and the failure of language as its means.

The endeavour to abolish metanarrative takes a different form with Stewart Parker, another explicitly *engagé* playwright to have treated the issue of collective identity in relation to the "Troubles." Parker's work unrelentingly undermines the discourse of identity by incessant theatrical experimentation and the deployment of fundamental playfulness. His aesthetic is outlined here through the juxtaposition of its principles with both the Romantic and the post-structuralist practice of irony. The thematic analysis of some of his plays provided within this context deals chiefly with Parker's central motif of ghosts, which, similarly to the drama itself, is subject to ongoing modification. The wild and oppressive dance and struggle of "ancestral wraiths"[6] is seen to build up to their final laying to rest as the only plausible source of hope. This liberation may, however, be achieved only by ultimately abandoning irony and relinquishing the former experimentation.

The concluding chapter deals with contemporary drama: the resilience of Irishness as a dominant theme within vigorous and assertive Celtic Tiger Ireland is documented by the success of Martin McDonagh. The present comments on his work stress McDonagh's stunning talent, yet at the same time point out the schematic nature of his theatrical enterprise. It is the ambivalent reception of McDonagh by Irish drama critics, however, that merits particular attention, since McDonagh's plays ultimately satirise the critical concern with Irish identity that is still quite pervasive. McDonagh paints an outrageous picture of rural Ireland and dares the critics to treat it as representational and take offence, while the radiant hyperbole makes the absurdity of such a stance manifest. The ironic appropriation of mainstream Irish drama from Synge to Tom Murphy and Friel and its generic blending with soap opera and the gangster movie only enhances the effect of the satire, while forming an essential part of the grotesque entertainment offered by the playwright.

As apparent from the outline above, this book does not aim at an exhaustive overview but the choice of playwrights and texts is selective. The gender imbalance in particular remains regrettable: for instance, early considerations of including a section on Marina Carr as part of the discussion of

---

6 Stewart Parker, Introduction to *Three Plays for Ireland* (London: Oberon Books, 1989) 9.

I. VISIONS

"The Home of Ancient Idealism": W.B. Yeats and the Irish Dramatic Movement

A few preliminary remarks are required concerning the present reading of what William Butler Yeats came to call "The Irish Dramatic Movement," its guiding metanarrative and the numerous ironic moments which intersperse and surround it. To begin with, the Dramatic Movement in fact comprised three successive—and distinct—theatrical projects: the Irish Literary Theatre (1899-1901), the Irish National Theatre Society (1903-1906) and the National Theatre Society, Ltd (founded in 1906). Despite the undeniable modifications of theatrical practice and repertoire, and the even more obvious changes with regard to membership and participation in these projects, a remarkable continuity may be observed among them. To a large extent, the continuity was defined by the ideas of W.B. Yeats and Lady Gregory (with Yeats authoring most of the articles and essays on the movement); hence, their views are treated in what follows as the most substantial component of the Dramatic Movement's metanarrative.

My approach tends to stress the essential coherence of the metanarrative. However, at the same time it is essential to bear in mind the incessant shifts of public rhetoric and the actual theatrical business of what eventually became the Irish national theatre. The metanarrative clearly underwent significant development over the formative decade or so: the early national theatre needs to be viewed first and foremost as a cultural nationalist project which happened within a highly polarised and a rapidly changing political context; much of the rhetorical manoeuvring with its frequent inconsistencies clearly took place chiefly as a result of this fact. Moreover, Yeats's political views seem to have changed considerably while the Dramatic Movement was under way—this may account for some further apparent contradictions. And finally, Yeats became involved in the movement as the author of many pronouncements on the theatre but only a few lyrical dramas, while having no professional experience in the theatre. Through participation in the staging of his plays, and by watching a significant amount of new European theatre, he began to grow into a major avant-garde playwright. This in turn influenced how he developed his writings on the Irish Dramatic Movement.

All in all, the complexity of the whole context is clearly evident, and a balanced perspective of the enterprise must take into account all the above aspects. From the onset, Yeats and his collaborators found themselves firmly embedded in an intricate network of forces involved in negotiations concerning the present and future shape of Irish cultural as well as political identity. My essay aims to discuss the effect of some of these forces on the statements of objectives and on some of the most prominent dramatic texts of the early national theatre, pointing out the accompanying ironic interaction between texts and contexts.

Representing the Nation

The idea of the Irish Literary Theatre was born out of a conversation between W.B. Yeats, Lady Gregory and Edward Martyn during their stay at Coole Park in August 1897.[1] Shortly afterwards, Yeats and Lady Gregory composed a letter and sent it out to prominent figures in Irish cultural life, announcing the

---

[1] R.F. Foster, *W.B. Yeats: A Life. I. The Apprentice Mage* (Oxford and New York: Oxford University Press, 1997) 183.

aims of the movement and soliciting support. This statement, later described by Lady Gregory as perhaps "a little pompous,"[2] went as follows:

> We propose to have performed in Dublin in the spring of every year certain Celtic and Irish plays, which whatever be their degree of excellence will be written with high ambition, and so to build up a Celtic and Irish school of dramatic literature. We hope to find in Ireland an uncorrupted and imaginative audience trained to listen by its passion for oratory, and believe that our desire to bring upon the stage the deeper thoughts and emotions of Ireland will ensure for us a tolerant welcome, and that freedom to experiment which is not found in theatres of England, and without which no new movement in art or literature can succeed. We will show that Ireland is not the home of buffoonery and of easy sentiment, as it has been represented, but the home of ancient idealism. We are confident of the support of all Irish people, who are weary of misrepresentation, in carrying out a work that is outside all the political questions that divide us.[3]

The dominant kind of drama which was to be found on the Irish stage at the time was indeed chiefly English popular melodrama, often rather sentimental, while Irish characters were mostly reduced to ridiculous caricatures.[4] The effort to eliminate this kind of misrepresentation of Ireland as "the home of buffoonery and easy sentiment" was quite understandable, and, in fact, the concern not only of those who formed the Irish Literary Theatre.[5] However, the aim of Yeats and Lady Gregory

---

2 Lady Augusta Gregory, *Our Irish Theatre: A Chapter of Autobiography* (Gerrards Cross: Colin Smythe, 1972) 20.

3 Gregory, *Our Irish Theatre*, 20.

4 For a detailed history of these characters, see G.C. Duggan's remarkable study *The Stage Irishman* (Dublin and Cork: The Talbot Press, 1937).

5 At around the same time, the Gaelic League was involved in the promotion of new drama written in Irish, an effort which was to promote the language and at the same time provide nationalist propaganda, while there were a number of important patriotic amateur groups and associations involved in producing new indigenous drama, often with a radical political intent. See also below, 21.

went far beyond a mere rectification of previous misrepresentations: they proposed to set up a theatre movement which would produce original dramatic texts that would above all be good literature. Moreover, they wanted to establish in Dublin an innovative, cutting-edge theatre which would allow for the "freedom to experiment" denied to Yeats, or for that matter any unconventional playwright or theatre practitioner, in London.[6]

For the authors of the fundraising letter quoted above, the notion of replacing misrepresentations of Ireland and the Irish clearly implied that the country was to be shown as "the home of ancient idealism." The concept is closely connected with what W.B. Yeats had been striving to achieve in his early poetry, i.e., to recreate the heroic and noble past of his country. This Golden Age was to be used as a basis and legitimising force for the emancipation of the Irish nation. Nevertheless, it is apparent that instead of re-presenting the Irish past, Yeats actually created a particular, highly idiosyncratic version of it in his work. At the risk of oversimplification, the Gaelic Ireland of his early writing is basically a pastoral realm, the home of a heroic society ruled by intellectualised aristocracy and governed by an ancient idealist "dream" which connects the people with timeless spiritual truths.

Yeats's sources and the way he worked with them very much prevented him from coming too close to historical reality. Most of the material concerning the Irish past was written in the

---

[6] One of Yeats's models for his "Irish" theatre was the Independent Theatre of London (founded in 1891), an enterprise which had been dwindling away at the time as it had not met the current expectations of critics and audiences alike. Yeats's own play, *The Land of Heart's Desire*, met with ridicule in London in 1894. Moreover, the puritanical atmosphere in Victorian England resulted in fairly rigid censorship of the theatre. Cf. James W. Flannery, *W.B. Yeats and the Idea of a Theatre. The Early Abbey Theatre in Theory and Practice* (1976; New Haven and London: Yale University Press, 1989) 126, 130-31. For the influence of Greek drama and Ibsen on the Irish Literary Theatre, see Foster, *W.B. Yeats: A Life*, I.208.

Irish language which Yeats never sufficiently mastered.[7] A lot of his work that builds on folklore is based on the tales collected by Lady Gregory in the West of Ireland. Barring the fact that a situation in which an English-speaking Ascendancy lady[8] solicits stories from mainly Irish-speaking Catholic tenant farmers certainly has its specifics (what kind of stories was she in fact given, and were they really told as they would be among the locals?), Lady Gregory actually used a largely artificial "Kiltartan" dialect of English for their translation. These 'translations' seem to have been dealt with by Yeats more or less as pure sources of a crystalline peasant culture. Moreover, many of his poems and plays based on the medieval Ulster Cycle stories draw merely on the English versions published by Standish James O'Grady, which, although influential at the time, can hardly be considered very accurate (if proof were needed, one needs to look no further than O'Grady's own annotations to his work: for example, "As to the manner of composition—I read all the old stories of Cuculain that I could find and the tale found here just *emerged* out of the consequent memories and meditations").[9]

Of course, a poet is not a historian or archivist, and may perhaps be pardoned for shaping the past according to specific intentions, concerns or poetic vision. There are several apparent reasons for the early Yeats's romanticising and idealising tendencies (in which he has, admittedly, many parallels in other

[7] Yeats was apparently not a very gifted student of languages. Despite his occasional comments about his effort to learn Irish, the language clearly eluded him. Foster, *W.B. Yeats: A Life*, I.195, 255.

[8] According to James Pethica, Lady Gregory herself did not learn Irish until 1898. James Pethica, "'A Young Man's Ghost': Lady Gregory and J.M. Synge," *Irish University Review* 34.1 (2004): 4.

[9] An annotation to a copy of *In the Gates of the North* (1901), quoted in W.J. Mc Cormack, *From Burke to Beckett. Ascendancy, Tradition and Betrayal in Literary History* (Cork: Cork University Press, 1994) 234; O'Grady's emphasis. The style of O'Grady's and other similar 'translations' of early Irish texts was later to become a rewarding target of satire for Irish-speaking writers like Flann O'Brien/ Myles na gCopaleen, particularly in *At Swim-Two-Birds* and *An Béal Bocht*.

European revivalist/nationalist authors): first of all, he saw himself as a national poet involved in a cultural resuscitation of his country. In addition, his view of history was deeply influenced by a life-long obsession with mysticism and the occult, a tendency which—as Marjorie Howes has recently demonstrated—must not be underestimated in any treatment of his work.[10] Many critics have also pointed out Yeats's personal situation as a poor descendant of a Protestant Ascendancy family whose natural inclination would have been to look into the past for the by-gone days of glory.[11]

Although in her 1913 autobiography Lady Gregory dissociated herself from the word "Celtic" in the Irish Literary Theatre 'manifesto'[12] and the term is almost entirely absent from Yeats's writings on the Dramatic Movement, Celticism unmistakably constituted another important influence on the notion of Ireland as "the home of ancient idealism." Yeats's early work displays a remarkable influence of Ernest Renan's and Matthew Arnold's ideas concerning the ancient poetic race of their imagination.[13] Moreover, in 1897, together with several

---

[10] See Marjorie Howes, *Yeats's Nations. Gender, Class, and Irishness* (Cambridge: Cambridge University Press, 1996).

[11] Adrian Frazier sums up Yeats's material situation and its possible influence on his work, while referring to previous discussions of this aspect. See *Behind the Scenes. Yeats, Horniman, and the Struggle for the Abbey Theatre* (Berkeley, Los Angeles and London: University of California Press, 1990) 36-41. Even more recently, Declan Kiberd has shown how Yeats constructed his own childhood according to his poetic vision in his writing, idealising the landscape and omitting in his autobiography the painful interaction with certain adults. Declan Kiberd, *Inventing Ireland. The Literature of the Modern Nation* (London: Vintage, 1996) 105-109.

[12] She claimed that the term had been put in for the sake of Fiona Macleod (the pen name of William Sharp), while Gregory herself "never quite understood the meaning of the 'Celtic Movement.'" Gregory, *Our Irish Theatre*, 20. In fact, Gregory wrote in a letter of 1898, i.e. prior to the official inauguration of their theatre, that she was glad that the "poor Sharp-ridden term" had been dropped. Foster, *W.B. Yeats: A Life*, I.197. Yeats came to prefer the term "Irish" over "Celtic" in his essays on the theatre, while the influence of Celticist notions arguably abates in his later work.

[13] Cf. Mc Cormack, *From Burke to Beckett*, 224-39.

friends and associates the poet embarked upon a major secret project which was to create a set of indigenous rituals for an Order of Celtic Mysteries; their objective was for the Order to become the true hub of the spiritual life of Ireland. Despite his apparent avoidance of Celticist notions in public, Yeats in fact continued drafting plans for this mystical order up to as late as 1902.[14] The sway of Celticism over the theatrical venture is documented further by Roy Foster, who points out that the original draft of the manifesto was entitled "The Celtic Theatre" and the theatre was renamed as "The Irish Literary Theatre" since this was considered conceptually less problematic and not so politically dangerous.[15]

To sum it up, the Irish "ancient idealism" was obviously a distinctive construct of the literati involved in the Dramatic Movement, in particular W.B. Yeats, crafted under the multiple influences outlined above. The situation is hardly different with other essentialist notions included in the Irish Literary Theatre manifesto: "the deeper thoughts and emotions of Ireland," or indeed the very term "Irish" are cultural fabrications of a similar kind (as indeed they would be in any other national context, past or present). Nevertheless, the Dramatic Movement presented itself as an effort which was to eradicate misrepresentation, which to many of its critics and audiences implied a claim to possessing knowledge of the essence of these concepts, or perhaps worse, an unabashed strife for hegemony in defining these terms. Not surprisingly, the result was often public uproar.

The amount of controversy that surrounded many of the productions of Yeats and Gregory's national theatre was caused by a number of additional factors. For some nationalists, it was enough that most leaders of both the Irish Literary Theatre and the Irish National Theatre Society were of the Protestant Ascendancy, and hence usurped the right to speak for a

---

[14] See Flannery, *W.B. Yeats and the Idea of a Theatre*, 63-65, 81-86, and Foster, *W.B. Yeats: A Life*, I.164, 180, 186ff.

[15] Foster, *W.B. Yeats: A Life*, I.184-85.

predominantly Catholic nation of farmers, workers and *petite bourgeoisie*. Others objected that what claimed to be a national theatre staged principally plays in the language of the English coloniser. Many reservations were also expressed regarding the apparent foreign influences in the plays produced, as radical nationalists claimed that Irish literature should not imitate any foreign models. However, what significantly contributed to the unrest and the prolonged battles in the press was the fact that the original statements of the group's intentions were regarded as an expression of an effort to create drama that would represent Ireland *as it was*, an effort which implied to many that the method employed would be realism. And whatever the controversial plays of Yeats and Synge were, they were not realist.[16]

The issue of realism emerged at quite an early stage in the debate. When challenged over the way Irish peasants were depicted in his play *The Countess Cathleen* (1899), Yeats ultimately closed the debate by saying that "his play, of course, was purely symbolic, and as such it must be regarded."[17] Although from a certain perspective this is undoubtedly true, his remark also served to avoid the problem. Putting the Irish "peasant" on stage was really one of Yeats's early objectives: in the second volume of *Samhain*, a publication he produced from 1901 to 1908 to comment on the Dramatic Movement, the poet claimed that to focus on "modern drama of society" would mean only doing badly what the English did well. The Irish should instead "busy [them]selves with poetry and the countryman."[18] The "countryman" was one of Yeats's most manifest intellectual creations. Yeats, of course, was not the only Irish revivalist to have promoted the Irish tenant farmer to the noble-sounding peasant: James Flannery has pointed out

[16] On the issue of realism in Synge's plays, see my discussion of Synge in the following chapter.

[17] "Irish Literary Theatre: Dinner at the Shelbourne Hotel," *Daily Express* 12 May 1899: 5-6; quoted in Frazier, *Behind the Scenes*, 12.

[18] *Samhain: 1902*, reprinted in W.B. Yeats, *Explorations* (New York: Macmillan, 1962) 95-97.

how a peculiar notion of the "holy peasant" was created in the 1890s from the ideas of the Young Irelanders, chiefly by the Gaelic League and the Catholic Church.[19] The tendency to view the country people as morally pure harbingers of poetry and ancient tradition was certainly not of Irish manufacture: it may be traced back through Renan's and Arnold's notions of the Celt, through, for example, the early English Romantic poets (perhaps its most remarkable expression is to be found in Wordsworth and Coleridge's Preface to *Lyrical Ballads*) down to the foundations laid by Johann Gottfried von Herder. Although the peasantry of *The Countess Cathleen* have much in common with the hallowed peasantry of the Catholic intellectuals (for instance, whatever their society may look like, it is clearly still preferable to the modern, industrialised corruption of the city), Yeats plainly transgressed when indicating in his play that Irish peasants had lapsed into spiritual poverty and essentially needed an aristocracy to save them. His peasantry was not perceived as a poetic creation but rather a gross misrepresentation.

As the attacks on the Dramatic Movement continued, Yeats elaborated his idea of what being faithful in representing one's subject meant. "Literature," he claimed, "is always personal, always one man's vision of the world, one man's experience [...],"[20] while finding an expression for this experience in an original language and style meant that the writer expressed the truth. Yeats went on to say:

---

[19] Flannery, *W.B. Yeats and the Idea of a Theatre*, 151. P.J. Mathews recently added a specific description of the way in which the notion was shaped in the 1899 debate over the Irish language. P.J. Mathews, *Revival. The Abbey Theatre, Sinn Féin, The Gaelic League and the Co-operative Movement* (Cork: Cork University Press/ Field Day, 2003) 43-44.

[20] "An Irish National Theatre," *Samhain: 1903*, reprinted in Yeats, *Explorations*, 115. This statement was written in anticipation of the premiere of J.M. Synge's controversial one-act play *In the Shadow of the Glen*. Foster, *W.B. Yeats: A Life*, I.291-92.

After all, is not the greatest play not the play that gives the sensation of an external reality but the play in which there is the greatest abundance of life itself, of the reality that is in our minds?[21]

Lady Gregory echoed the sentiment later in the same year when facing objections to her play, *Spreading the News*, hoping that the Abbey Theatre audience was now sufficiently educated to know that "the much misquoted 'mirror to nature' was not used by [the play's] author or any good play-writer at all."[22] Yeats however simultaneously developed a line of argument which seemed to contradict the above: he kept on insisting that plays should be using real peasant characters, a language that would be "live" (i.e., based on the country idiom), and should depict "life in its daily aspects."[23] Incongruously perhaps, Yeats wanted to produce poetic, highly symbolic drama, but at the same time he believed that the drama should feature realistic rural characters (without acknowledging that these characters within the genre necessarily turn into imaginary beings). To an extent, his paradoxical argumentation may be seen as a response to a political context in which—as mentioned above—the idea of national drama implied staging realist plays (which would besides depict the Irish in a way acceptable to all kinds of nationalists).

[21] "The Play, The Player, and the Scene," *Samhain: 1904*, reprinted in Yeats, *Explorations*, 167.

[22] Gregory, *Our Irish Theatre*, 91. Quoted and discussed in Lionel Pilkington, *Theatre and the State in Twentieth-Century Ireland. Cultivating the People* (London and New York: Routledge, 2001) 69.

[23] *Samhain: 1905*, reprinted in Yeats, *Explorations*, 189. The language of drama is discussed in virtually every issue of *Samhain*. See, again, the preface to *Lyrical Ballads*: Version 1800—"to make the incidents of common life interesting," and especially Version 1802—"to chuse incidents and situations from common life, and to relate or describe them, throughout, as far as possible, in a selection of language really used by men." William Wordsworth and Samuel Taylor Coleridge, *Lyrical Ballads 1798*, ed. W.J.B. Owen (London: Oxford University Press, 1967) 156 and n11.

The issue of what exactly made a "national play" for Yeats is not uncomplicated either. Adrian Frazier has listed in his splendid study of the early national theatre six different concepts of a desirable Irish national theatre that were current at the time. These ranged from the production of Irish-language plays Catholic in morals (D.P. Moran), through subsidised native entertainment supervised by the Church (the owner of tramways and Catholic nationalist dailies W.M. Murphy), folk theatre inciting a revolt against British tyranny (Maud Gonne), Irish-language plays modelled on modern foreign drama such as that of Ibsen (G.J. Watson and other Dublin members of the Gaelic League), anything written by an Irish author that might be considered a work of art (a view advocated by many Home Rule Protestants, for instance, John Butler Yeats, the poet's father), to rather sentimental plays in English that upheld a particular "lofty view of the Irish character" (the largest group of nationalists following the legacy of the Young Ireland writers).[24] It was within this set of conflicting views that Yeats and his collaborators had to operate; in truth, the debate itself actually arose chiefly as a result of their dramatic activities.

Yeats's own idea of national drama was, broadly speaking, one of high art on "Irish subjects." He asserted that theatre should be predominantly "a place of intellectual excitement" producing "truth and beauty," i.e., something that is "above judgment" and has "no need of justification."[25] As for the criteria of what exactly made 'high art,' these seemed to Yeats largely self-evident. Clearly, there appeared to be those with an insight in the matter, and those without. Moreover, in a conversation on the issue to Lady Gregory, the poet showed no scruples about his method of demonstrating to his compatriots

---

[24] Frazier, *Behind the Scenes*, 100-104.
[25] "The Reform of the Theatre," *Samhain: 1903*, reprinted in Yeats, *Explorations*, 107.

what was good in aesthetic terms: "In questions of taste, it's no good to use argument, one must use force."[26]

When eventually pressed to justify his idea of "truth and beauty," having been challenged again by nationalist critics on the use of foreign influences, Yeats rather reluctantly produced a definition of "national literature":

> [National literature] is the work of writers who are moulded by influences that are moulding their country, and who write out of so deep a life that they are accepted there in the end.[27]

Although it may seem perhaps a trifle facile, one cannot help but note that what Yeats carefully condemns throughout his writing on Irish theatre are any *English* influences (exhibiting his talent for political correctness) which could nonetheless justifiably be seen as "moulding the country" to a major degree as well.[28] In any case, when addressing the views of those of his critics who were in favour of schematic drama, be it for the purpose of propaganda, popular entertainment or education in the Irish language, Yeats rightly claimed that "A nation is injured by the picking out of a single type and setting that into print or upon the stage as a type of the whole nation."[29] This is why the Stage Irishman was not to be replaced by a type of a virtuous patriot; instead, the world should be presented with the image of "the great writer of the nation."[30] And it did not matter greatly, Yeats finally admitted, that this writer may misrepresent "the average life of a nation," since that simply "follows of necessity from an imaginative delight in energetic

---

[26] Lady Gregory, *Seventy Years: Being the Autobiography of Lady Gregory*, ed. Colin Smythe (Gerrards Cross: Colin Smythe, 1973) 351.

[27] "First Principles," *Samhain: 1904*, reprinted in Yeats, *Explorations*, 156.

[28] At the same time, Yeats does not seem to regard Shakespeare and a few other canonical greats as English at all in this context, i.e., *their* influence is laudable.

[29] *Samhain: 1905*, reprinted in Yeats, *Explorations*, 191.

[30] *Samhain: 1905*, 192.

characters and extreme types" and in its effect "enlarges the energy of a people by the spectacle of energy."[31]

An Irish national writer, then, should provide the nation with pure art full of life and power, while mimetic accuracy should not really be an issue. This elaboration of the original manifesto amounts to a contradiction again, as the manifesto implies that representing Ireland as "the home of ancient idealism" means representing it correctly. The inconsistency itself does not necessarily have to suggest dishonesty on the part of Yeats: he himself as a writer would have been guided— if a degree of simplification may be pardoned—by a vision of his native land as a realm of genuine and timeless poetry. Moreover, Marjorie Howes has pointed out the highly idiosyncratic nature of Yeats's concept of the nation: under the influence of his occult studies, Yeats thought of the nation as a group of autonomous individuals who together formed a greater collective mind in which their perspectives complemented one another in perfect harmony.[32] Viewed in this light, many an apparent contradiction in Yeats's articles on the theatre ceases to be problematic. Nonetheless, Yeats's idea of the nation was hardly available (and, for that matter, acceptable) to his readers and audience. From that perspective, his statements continue to resonate with paradox.

The shifts in viewpoint and changes of stress in Yeats's comments on the national theatre were also connected with matters of theatrical practice. Yeats's initial thoughts continued to develop not only under the influence of the controversies created by the productions of the Irish Literary Theatre and the Irish National Theatre Society, but were also shaped by his growing experience as a theatre practitioner. One does not need to agree with Adrian Frazier who suggests that Yeats would have been initially quite unclear about what he wanted to

[31] *Samhain: 1905*, 191.
[32] Howes, *Yeats's Nations*, 87-88.

[23]

achieve in his Dublin theatre project.[33] However, there certainly was a difference between the Yeats of 1898 who essentially lacked playwrights, actors and theatre alike and was planning to stir things up by producing experimental plays, thereby encouraging new Irish writing compatible with his aesthetic demands, and the Yeats of 1906 who had succeeded in making 'his' theatre a focal point of cultural debate, gained a number of gifted authors and practitioners as collaborators, participated in the process of staging some of the plays and had been given a theatre by Miss Annie Horniman. Frazier is certainly correct in stressing that to promote an independent artistic theatre was a different matter indeed when it was done from this position.[34]

Teaching the Audience

When examining the situation of the Dramatic Movement in the web of cultural and political negotiations, it is important to note how Yeats and Lady Gregory perceived their audience. The 'manifesto' is clear in its hopes for "an uncorrupted and imaginative audience trained to listen by its passion for oratory," and voices confidence in a general "support of all Irish people, who are weary of misrepresentation." From the onset, however, these beliefs proved to be rather misguided. As mentioned above, a wide controversy arose around the first production of the Irish Literary Theatre, *The Countess Cathleen*, and attacks were repeated regularly with many subsequent plays—Yeats's *The Hour-Glass* (1903) and *The King's Threshold* (1903), for instance—while protests against J.M. Synge's plays eventually turned into a full-fledged riot over *The Playboy of the Western World* (1907). While there had been some hope for imaginative reception, or at least mere tolerance, the actual response was often very different indeed.

---

[33] Frazier, *Behind the Scenes*, Ch. 2. Foster has produced a detailed analysis which insists on the firmness of Yeats's intentions. See *W.B. Yeats: A Life*, I. Ch. 7.
[34] Frazier, *Behind the Scenes*, 105.

This would have only reinforced the condescending view Ascendancy artists such as Yeats and Lady Gregory had of the Catholic majority of the Irish. It is remarkable to observe how often Yeats when facing a conflict described his audience as a "mob," while both he and Lady Gregory tended to label audience protests as "riots."[35] Clearly, the audiences somehow did not have the right to protest, and if they did, they were seen as a mere bunch of ignorant barbarians. In Frazier's words, "one must remember that Yeats was a nationalist but not a democrat,"[36] and in matters of art, Lady Gregory was as elitist as Yeats. The enterprise of the theatre was perceived by both its leaders as essentially didactic: drama was to provide aesthetic education, and the experience of it was to transform a mob into a nation.[37] Indeed, Foster shows that Yeats conceived of drama as a way of preaching which was to educate and unite the people.[38] This idea is in turn quite consistent with Howes's assertion that Yeats intended the Irish Literary Theatre to provide an "alternative mass culture"[39] which was to replace the abject popular entertainment brought over from Britain. Documents proving the educative drive of the Dramatic Movement's leaders abound. To cite a single outstanding instance, Lady Gregory complained in a letter to Yeats about the lack of the didactic element in some of the plays they had just produced and added a spectacularly condescending remark: "We have been humouring our audience instead of

---

[35] Lionel Pilkington, "'Every Crossing Sweeper Thinks Himself a Moralist': The Critical Role of Audiences in Irish Theatre History," *Irish University Review* 27.1 (1997): 154-55. Despite her ambivalent feelings about Synge, Lady Gregory wrote about him as a master dramatist facing a mob, while Yeats famously glorified Synge along similar lines in his essay "Synge and the Ireland of His Time." Cf. Pilkington, *Theatre and the State*, 67.

[36] Frazier, *Behind the Scenes*, 17.

[37] Howes has pointed out in this context Yeats's favourite misquotation of Victor Hugo: "in the theatre the mob bec[omes] a people." Howes, *Yeats's Nations*, 71-72, 87-88.

[38] Foster, *W.B. Yeats: A Life*, I.213-14.

[39] Howes, *Yeats's Nations*, 68.

educating it. [...] It is the old battle between those who use a toothbrush and those who don't."[40]

Lionel Pilkington has recently made the instructive impulse of the early national theatre a central thesis in a challenging book; in an earlier article he stressed that in fact all of Lady Gregory's 1913 autobiography "tells a story of an Irish audience's self-education."[41] This pedagogical tendency received notable public confirmation when Yeats delivered his legendary speeches during the riots against *The Playboy of the Western World,* and later O'Casey's *The Plough and the Stars,* and accused the audience of having "disgraced" themselves.

It is undeniable that Yeats and Gregory remarkably stood their ground even in the fiercest battles with their audiences, and often seemed to risk the very existence of the theatre itself. Ironically, however, this prolonged struggle—together with what he perceived as the lack of public understanding of his own plays—has also led the national writer Yeats to eventually turn as a dramatist towards "an unpopular theatre and an audience like a secret society,"[42] where admission would be strictly regulated and no one would dispute the relevance of the plays' meaning.[43] Apparently, as far as Yeats was concerned, the didactic mission of the Irish Dramatic Movement had failed.

Many pages have been written about how incredibly skilful, or alternately cunning and ruthless Yeats was when positioning himself and his projects in the discourse of Irish culture and politics. On the one hand, some splendid new writing was both produced and encouraged, cultural institutions were established and made to flourish; on the other hand, friends were insulted and abandoned, including those whose generosity had been useful in the past, and a few talented

---

[40] Quoted in Pilkington, "'Every Crossing Sweeper,'" 155.

[41] Pilkington, *Theatre and the State.* Pilkington, "'Every Crossing Sweeper,'" 155.

[42] W.B. Yeats, "A People's Theatre" (1919), reprinted in Yeats, *Explorations,* 254.

[43] Although Yeats may in fact be seen as merely reviving an intention he had before the Irish Dramatic Movement went under way: one of his early plans had been to set up a small group producing poetic theatre in London. The plan had failed. See, for instance, Frazier, *Behind the Scenes,* 45ff.

authors were suppressed, be it for private reasons or possibly even out of artistic rivalry. Yeats's manipulations during the struggle for his idea of the national theatre were, of course, no exception. The present analysis of the guiding metanarrative of the Irish Dramatic Movement and its modifications will be best served at this point by examining two of its important early productions: *The Countess Cathleen* and *Cathleen ni Houlihan*.

The Objectionable Countess

Yeats's *The Countess Cathleen* gave rise to the first storm.[44] In fact, the launch of the theatre by this production was deliberately orchestrated by Yeats and poet George Russell (AE) as controversial: Yeats and Russell provoked in particular a strident debate with John Eglinton in the Dublin *Express* over the desired nature of national drama, which was to serve as a prelude to the first season of the Irish Literary Theatre.[45] The atmosphere of general curiosity created by this debate was notoriously seized upon by one F. Hugh O'Donnell (an ill-famed malcontent with a score to settle with Yeats) who circulated around Dublin a pamphlet entitled "Souls for Gold" shortly before the premiere of 8 May 1899. In this he asserted that *The Countess Cathleen* was grossly immoral and that it distorted the character of the Irish peasant. An open letter by a group of students from the new Catholic university appeared in the press in anticipation of the play, again denouncing its immorality.[46] Consequently, the audience can hardly be said to

---

[44] W.B. Yeats, *Collected Works II: The Plays*, eds. David R. Clark and Rosalind E. Clark (Houndmills and New York: Palgrave, 2001) 27-63. The edition includes extensive annotations regarding the numerous changes made by Yeats over several decades after he completed the first version of the play in 1892. A detailed summary of all the events and objections to the play is to be found in Frazier, *Behind the Scenes*, 1-23.

[45] Foster, *W.B. Yeats: A Life*, I.197-98.

[46] Mathews, *Revival*, 55. The students wrote their letter on the basis of an early version of the play which was significantly different from the text performed on the opening night. See Joan FitzPatrick Dean, *Riot and Great Anger. Stage*

have arrived in the theatre unbiased. Indeed, many people came with a clear purpose, be it to defend the Catholic faith and their view of the Irish nation (mainly the militant Catholic students), or to support the freedom of the arts (another group of students from the Catholic university who refused to sign their classmates' letter came to support the play loudly, James Joyce among them), or indeed merely to witness what would happen. The result, predictably, was a performance accompanied by hisses, boos and cheers, while one can only wonder, along with Frazier, how much of the play would have actually been *heard* by the audience.[47] Finally, Cardinal Logue condemned *The Countess Cathleen* two days after the opening night on the basis of O'Donnell's pamphlet, admittedly without having read or seen the play, and thus aggravated the controversy even further.[48]

Radical Catholic nationalists raised a set of objections against the play text. To begin with, the very title of the play clearly associated the allegorical woman of Ireland with the aristocracy; as Howes puts it, *The Countess Cathleen* drew "resolutely on nationalist traditions that were anti-Ascendancy in order to promote Ascendancy interests."[49] Worse still, the play depicted the aristocracy as better and of more value than the farmers, and that even applied in the afterlife, as the price for the soul of the Countess offered by the demons significantly differed from those quoted for the souls of her tenants. This was clearly unacceptable to the Catholic majority in general, both for political and religious reasons: the superiority of the Ascendancy was simply intolerable, and, according to the Catholic doctrine, the price of people was equal in the eyes of God. The alleged moral superiority of the aristocracy was furthermore highlighted in the play by the fact that the farmers

Censorship in Twentieth-Century Ireland (Madison and London: The University of Wisconsin Press, 2004) 53.

[47] Frazier, *Behind the Scenes*, 21.

[48] Dean, *Riot and Great Anger*, 54.

[49] Howes, *Yeats's Nations*, 47.

were by and large ready to sell their souls to the Devil,[50] while the Countess did so only after she had given away all her property to the starving people, and only as a sacrifice for their sake. Her gesture was finally commended by God, and the Countess was restored to her position on earth. Apart from the idea of the aristocracy's superiority, Frazier is quite correct in suggesting that the play's setting at the time of a famine must have awoken memories of the Great Famine of 1846-47, while the celebration of the generosity of the landlord in the play principally meant "turning a Protestant moral catastrophe into a miracle of benevolence."[51]

Yeats immediately found himself having to defend the kind of picture of Irish history that the play painted, and—as noted earlier—decided to shift the debate into the much safer realm of aesthetics, claiming that the play was a symbolic work of art and as such did not bear any direct relevance to reality. This happened at a gala dinner organised to celebrate the controversy.[52] The 'battle' over the play was indeed eventually won by Yeats, while the debate gradually turned into one concerned almost entirely with the freedom of artistic expression. However, the author of *The Countess Cathleen* was made painfully aware that the gaze of the audience and critics alike was firmly focused on the issue of 'correct' representation of the country, insisting first on checking the verisimilitude of the piece rather than pondering any complex symbols. Consequently, Yeats only then started to elaborate on what it actually meant to rectify "misrepresentations" of a country, which inevitably led him to write extensively about such matters as the nature of truth in literature. This line of thought, definitely encouraged by further cultural skirmishes, eventually made him express his views in statements asserting that truth

[50] Yeats was shrewd enough to drop an additional objectionable detail from the play—a moment in which an Irish peasant is shown to kick a Marian shrine to pieces. Pilkington, *Theatre and the State*, 224n1.

[51] Frazier, *Behind the Scenes*, 14.

[52] Foster, *W.B. Yeats: A Life*, I.211.

[29]

was a "self-consistent personal vision" and not a "historical and external" matter.[53] When used as a supplement to the original manifesto of the theatre, statements like this make it seem a very different text indeed.

In terms of the Irish Literary Theatre's PR, the play was a "howling success."[54] In comparison with the later *Playboy* riots, the protests in the theatre were relatively innocuous, while the fact that the play had been denounced from the pulpit brought people flocking in to see it.[55] Apart from that, the extent to which some nationalist papers supported the play despite having reservations about its content was surprising (as Pilkington points out). What mattered most for them was that Yeats and his collaborators intended to encourage new Irish writing of tolerable artistic quality for the stage.[56]

Lady Gregory later quoted as proof of the play's success that when it was revived at the Abbey in 1911, there were no protests any more, and characteristically added that the audience had learnt their lesson.[57] However, a better way of putting it is to say that the play was just "tolerated"[58] by the Abbey audiences. By this stage, the original dispute was well exhausted, the reasons for coming to see the performance would undoubtedly have been chiefly different, while there were new plays to fight over. In fact, the moderate success of *The Countess Cathleen* in its revivals in the first decade of the century does not necessarily say very much even of its literary, and certainly not its dramatic quality. *The Countess Cathleen* manifestly betrays the lack of experience of practical theatre on the part of its author: much of the dialogue is too complex and undramatic, while the Wagnerian final scene in particular appears to be almost unstageable. These features were

53 W.B. Yeats, "On Taking the *Playboy* to London" (1907), reprinted in *Explorations*, 230.
54 James Cousins quoted in Foster, *W.B. Yeats: A Life*, I.212.
55 Dean, *Riot and Great Anger*, 57.
56 Pilkington, *Theatre and the State*, 8.
57 Gregory, *Our Irish Theatre*, 25.
58 Frazier, *Behind the Scenes*, 20.

highlighted even further in the original production which must have been simply terrible. The small space of the Antient Concert Rooms was hardly adequate for a play of such sweeping scope and the means available for mounting the production were limited (as a result, the stage decor and effects were dangerously close to the worst kind of amateur theatre). Moreover, English actors were hired for the play (another error committed by Yeats in the eyes of the nationalists) who could not pronounce most of the Irish names correctly.[59] The 1911 revival of the play had at any rate the advantage that Yeats was by then much more skilled in the craft of playwriting, and had also encountered Gordon Craig and reshaped the play under his influence. At least one later critic has called the result "impressive."[60]

The Shan Van Vocht

Of all plays produced by the early national theatre, it was *Cathleen ni Houlihan* (1902) that met with the warmest reception from nationalist audience members.[61] Co-written by Yeats and Lady Gregory, it is a short, predominately prose piece, with a clear political message. It is exactly the kind of drama that one would expect when viewing the intentions of the theatre group through the eyes of a fervent patriot. At the same time, it is the very opposite of what one would envisage when reading Yeats's statements about staying apolitical and producing art with no immediate relevance to reality. Many people who saw Maud Gonne's evocative performance as the allegorical woman of Ireland reported how they felt moved to take immediate action (the critic Stephen Gwynn later wondered whether "such plays should be produced unless one was prepared for people

---

[59] A detailed analysis of this dramatic failure is to be found in Flannery, *W.B. Yeats and the Idea of a Theatre*, 144-49. His book is my main source on the original production.

[60] Flannery, *W.B. Yeats and the Idea of a Theatre*, 273.

[61] Yeats, *Collected Works II: The Plays*, 83-93.

to go out to shoot and be shot"),[62] while leaders of the 1916 Rising Padraic Pearse and Constance Markievicz claimed to have been deeply affected and inspired by the play. Even Yeats himself famously mused in a later poem: "Did that play of mine send out/ Certain men the English shot?"[63] Be that as it may, what a curious change of direction this seems to suggest.

In order to understand why this occurred, one must again examine the context in which the play was written. Adrian Frazier has poignantly shown that after the controversy over *The Countess Cathleen* Yeats found himself in a situation which threatened to deprive him of most of his nationalist audience.[64] At the same time, he finally managed to target a promising group of Irish actors, the Fay brothers and their Irish National Dramatic Company, whose services he wanted to use in his future productions (while he already had a promise of funding). The Fays' idea of a national theatre significantly differed from his in that they basically wanted it to produce—at least at that moment in time—mainly short, uncomplicated miracle plays about major political issues, with an unambiguous impact on the audience.

Yeats first of all needed to re-establish the credentials he lost with the nationalists after *The Countess Cathleen*.[65] In March and April 1900 he wrote a series of letters to the press in which he attacked the current visit of Queen Victoria to Ireland; this move resulted, as a side-effect perhaps, in a prominent Loyalist supporter of the Irish Literary Theatre, the Trinity College historian Lecky resigning publicly from the theatre's board.[66] When challenged some months later on the issue of national

[62] Stephen Gwynn, *Irish Literature and Drama in the English Language: A Short History* (New York: Thomas Nelson and Sons, 1936) 158-59; quoted in Pilkington, '"Every Crossing Sweeper,"' 152.

[63] W.B. Yeats, "The Man and the Echo" (1939), *Collected Poems*, ed. Augustine Martin (London: Vintage, 1992) 361.

[64] Frazier, *Behind the Scenes*, 56-59.

[65] Cf. Pilkington, *Theatre and the State*, 29.

[66] A detailed discussion of Yeats's manoeuvrings is to be found in Frazier, *Behind the Scenes*, 25-31.

the extent that none of his subsequent plays became instantly popular.

This hostility could be attributed simply to the fact that Synge's plays plainly offended the nationalist idea of the virtuous and heroic Irishwoman and Irishman; however, the issue is rather more complex. Even without subscribing to a version of dogmatic nationalism, the audience would have been legitimate in criticising Synge for the way Ireland was represented in his drama, simply due to the fact that he staged his plays as part of a movement claiming to rectify misrepresentations of the country on the platform of an Irish national theatre.

In the previous chapter, we noted that the idea of representing Ireland in a true manner seemed to imply realism as the method used; and realism is certainly *one* of the modes employed in Synge's plays. In fact, with his early plays, Synge rather meticulously insisted on realistic detail on the stage. The interior of the cottage in *The Shadow of the Glen* was modelled on a real cottage in Glenmalure, for instance, while the author was also very particular about where individual objects should be placed. The props for *Riders to the Sea* were gathered around the Irish countryside, while Synge even had a pair of pampooties— the traditional Aran footwear—sent over to Dublin, together with a sample of Aran flannel, for everything to look completely genuine. (He later proceeded to urge his beloved Molly Allgood to learn spinning "so that there be no fake about the show.")[3] Ann Saddlemyer has quite poignantly described the effect of such realist detail: "it is hardly surprising [...] that the audience, taken off guard by the realism of the production in front of them, should take the next step and accept literally the words and situation presented there."[4] Despite this, there is

---

[3] See Ann Saddlemyer's introduction to Synge's *Collected Works III: Plays, Book 1*, ed. Ann Saddlemyer (Oxford: Oxford University Press, 1968; Gerrards Cross: Colin Smythe/ Washington: The Catholic University of America Press, 1982) xviii-xix.

[4] Saddlemyer, Introduction to Synge, *Collected Works*, III.xix.

no doubt that Synge's plays are far from being documentary snapshots of Irish country life. Anthropological and/or antiquarian concerns are rarely present, while realist detail forms merely a deceptive surface. The core of the meaning is clearly to be found elsewhere.

Synge has also been challenged for the way he treated the language of the Irish peasants in his plays. In fact, the initial objections to the language of Synge's characters gave rise to a critical debate that divided scholars into two camps for a long time: those claiming that Synge copied (and thus preserved) the idiom of the Irish peasants and those claiming his language was entirely synthetic. Most early adherents to the latter view tended to assert that Synge's language was therefore fundamentally flawed because of its inauthenticity. It was only in the 1970s that Nicholas Grene and Katharine Worth discussed the syntheticity in terms of original artistic creation.[5]

One issue that had never been addressed in the early criticism was crucial: was it a rural dialect of Hiberno-English that Synge was supposed to be representing, or rather the Irish language of the West of Ireland, particularly the Aran Islands? If it were the latter, translation would be implied in the process of composition, a fact that would problematise the very essence of the debate about Synge's authenticity.

In the introduction to his pioneering study, *Synge and the Irish Language* (1979), Declan Kiberd noted the main reason for such a significant flaw in the critical debate. Up until the late 1970s, there had been no critic of Synge with a sufficient knowledge of the Irish language, while such knowledge was undeniably essential to any deeper analysis of the language of Synge's works.[6] Kiberd demonstrated in his book how

---

[5] Grene and Worth have also contributed significantly to the view of Synge as a European rather than merely Irish Revivalist playwright. Cf. Nicholas Grene, *Synge: A Critical Study of the Plays* (London and Basingstoke: Macmillan, 1975); and Katharine Worth, *The Irish Drama of Europe from Yeats to Beckett* (London: The Athlone Press, 1978), Ch. 5.

[6] Declan Kiberd, *Synge and the Irish Language*, 2nd ed. (Dublin: Gill and Macmillan, 1993) 2.

profoundly Synge was influenced by Irish: he habitually put down particular expressions in his notebooks and then imported them into his plays, or often took phrases from letters written to him in Irish, translated them literally into English and then used them in his drama.[7] Kiberd also pointed out that the passages in *The Playboy* which were criticised as too exotic or extravagant were in fact based on Irish courtly love poetry, and that this was also where the references in the play to the Ancient Greeks and Romans came from.[8]

On the other hand, Kiberd was also one of several critics to have shown the extent to which Synge was influenced—in the same way as many other contemporaries—by the particular brand of Hiberno-English developed by Douglas Hyde in his translations of Irish-language poetry.[9] Synge was, moreover, quite diligent in recording in his notebooks individual turns of phrase used in the English of Irish country people, be it in Wicklow, Kerry, Connemara or the Aran Islands. Despite the fact that Kiberd was the first to plausibly discuss the actual influence of the Irish language on the playwright, he did not join the camp of those who claimed Synge to be a preserver of an existing and pure country idiom. In his book, Kiberd joins proponents of Synge's syntheticism such as Grene or Worth; he demonstrates that the playwright was a compiler who drew from different linguistic sources in order to create a very specific idiom of his own.

Apart from being an original assemblage of sources, the language of Synge's drama is also highly rhythmical and melodic, and frequently features alliteration. As a matter of fact,

---

7 Kiberd, *Synge and the Irish Language*, 206-7.
8 Kiberd, *Synge and the Irish Language*, 122-40.
9 Kiberd, *Synge and the Irish Language*, 129-46, and Kiberd, *Inventing Ireland*, 153. Hyde's short plays in Irish represent another crucial influence on Synge: Hyde may be credited with introducing on the Irish stage (e.g., in *The Tinker and the Sheeog* or *The Twisting of the Rope*) the figure of the solitary, poetic tramp which then became central to most of Synge's drama (and by further extension, the work of Beckett). Cf. also Kiberd, *Synge and the Irish Language*, 146-50 and Flannery, *W.B. Yeats and the Idea of a Theatre*, 172.

this was illustrated even by opponents of the playwright who parodied his plays in the language of his characters. Synge's poeticising tendency perceptibly progresses with each new play. Several studies have demonstrated Synge's deliberation and skill when working both with sound patterns and rhythm. While regular patterns of sound appear as a significant element in all of Synge's plays, a development can be traced regarding the rhythmical patterns. The rhythm in the early plays is often broken; however, in *The Well of the Saints* it achieves an almost complete regularity. This regularity is then strategically broken in particular dialogues of *The Playboy* in order to prevent a threatening monotony.[10] Synge's language has indeed been likened to music.[11] Needless to say, arguments to the effect that the playwright only copied badly a genuine idiom appear plainly ridiculous in the face of Synge's meticulous work with sound and rhythm and the fact that no people on earth really speak in regular poetic cadences embellished with recurrent sound patterns.

Synge's attitude to the language he employed was quite typical of the reclusive satirist and poet, and as a matter of fact closely resembled his approach to the issue of realism. Take the much-quoted statement from the preface to *The Playboy*:

[10] A detailed analysis of rhythm in Synge appears in Uwe Stork, *Der sprachliche Rhythmus in den Bühnenstücken John Millington Synges*, inaugural dissertation (Freiburg i. Br.: n.p., 1969), which is also my main source here. A discussion of Synge's rhythm is to be found also in Hugh Kenner, "The Living World of the Text: The Playboy" (1983), *John Millington Synge's The Playboy of the Western World*, ed. Harold Bloom (New York: Chelsea House, 1988) 126-29; and P.L. Henry, "The Playboy of the Western World," *Philologica Pragensia* 3 (1965): 198-204. Synge's use of specific rhythmical patterns often finds reflection in translations of the plays into other languages: for instance, a recent translation of The Playboy into Czech attempted to convey the melodicity of the language essentially by using the iambic rhythm of the blank verse. J.M. Synge, *Hrdina západu*, trans. Martin Hilský (Praha: Národní divadlo, 1996). The translator's analysis of rhythm in the play is outlined in a supplementary essay entitled "Poznámka o překladu" (70-79).

[11] Worth, *The Irish Drama of Europe*, 123.

intentions are best left alone, and with someone as elusive as Synge doubly so.

The Wife of Glenmalure: The Shadow of the Glen

The hostile reaction to Synge's first play to be staged, *(In) The Shadow of the Glen*, has already been mentioned, together with the context in which it occurred. In a poignant discussion of the first production of the play, Adrian Frazier has suggested that the concern with the expected misrepresentation of the Irish on the stage would have been further enhanced by several other, supposedly extrinsic elements, such as the seating arrangement and the acting in individual roles. The INTS were faced on the opening night with an unexpected visit of the British Chief Secretary of Ireland at the time, George Wyndham, who was seated in a red armchair, while across the aisle from him the senior Fenian John O'Leary was sitting in a normal seat, to one side. Consequently, even the actors themselves felt that "the wrong man was in the red chair," and that the royal treatment given to the British officials was somewhat dubious. Moreover, the rendering of Nora by Maire nic Shiublaigh was apparently rather "erotically charged," making the character more of a bad wife than a courageous heroine, while on the other hand, W.G. Fay's Dan Burke was far too comic for the audience to see him as a spiteful and oppressive old man.[33]

The individual objections to the play have been treated at length by others;[34] I shall thus confine myself merely to a brief summary here. The atmosphere before the premiere was similar to that preceding the opening night of *The Countess Cathleen*: word got round about how outrageous the depiction of rural life apparently was in the play, an article was published in the *Irish Daily Independent* accusing the company of perverting the aims it had declared, and the secession from the company of

[33] Frazier, *Behind the Scenes*, 73-74.
[34] For a synopsis of previous discussions of these, and for a useful recent analysis, see Frazier, *Behind the Scenes*, 80-87.

prominent supporters and actors was announced.[35] After the first performance, the play's detractors maintained that *The Shadow of the Glen* scandalised Irish women, who according to them were "the most virtuous [...] in the world"[36] and would never consider leaving their husband and walking out with a tramp. Moreover, Arthur Griffith and others saw the play as not based on Irish experience or folklore but derived from the tale "The Widow of Ephesus," versions of which are to be found in Petronius and Boccaccio. Despite the fact that Yeats came to Synge's defence, claiming that the story had been narrated to the author on the Aran Islands, and that Synge even later attempted to publish the Aran narrative during a renewed controversy over the play,[37] the allegation that he modelled his play on foreign sources had never entirely been withdrawn. Ironically, it seemed to matter little that the ending of the play was really very different from the story of the Widow of Ephesus, or indeed any similar folk tale, as the unfaithful wife who is put to an extreme test by a suspicious husband is inevitably punished for her behaviour, while in Synge's play she comes out victorious (albeit perhaps only in a moral sense).

Griffith's choice of argument is in fact quite revealing. The story of the bad wife and the husband pretending to be dead was well known in Irish folklore at the time,[38] while also being, of course, part of a wider European legacy. Not only did Griffith choose to ignore the existence and familiarity of the tale in Ireland, but he also decided to chastise Synge for referring to its European versions elaborated by those he saw as notoriously bacchanalian authors. The argument appears to have been a mere surrogate for the real problem, which consisted in the final twist introduced to the narrative by Synge. This twist— together with the heroine's name (this with a rather

---

35 Dean, *Riot and Great Anger*, 74.
36 Arthur Griffith, *The United Irishman* 10.243 (24 Oct. 1903): 2.
37 *The United Irishman* (11 Feb. 1905) published only Synge's letter accompanying the source text. Cf. Synge, *Collected Works*, III: "Appendix B," 254.
38 Pilkington, *Theatre and the State*, 40.

mischievous ambivalence, as Nora happens to be a very common Irish name)—Synge clearly borrowed from Ibsen,[39] who was regarded at the time as an utter abomination by most Irish writers on the national literature. Curiously enough, this particular "foreign influence" was never stressed by Griffith.

All in all, reviewers and protesters alike were united in that a naturalist story of an oppressed wife and her bleak living conditions, together with her path to liberation by embracing the poetic world of a romanticised tramp, definitely had no place in their notion of the Irish dramatic canon. What is important to note though is that almost without exception, the objections raised were clearly connected with the specific context of the first (and second) production of the play. The same obviously applies to contributing factors such as acting styles. When circumstances changed, that is, mainly when Synge's work ceased to be regarded as erroneous realism, the reception of the play became remarkably less hostile. Whatever later audiences may have thought of the chastity of Irish women, they did not perceive it as relevant to the play's meaning.

Apart from the ironies *vis-à-vis* the proclaimed intentions of the Irish Literary Theatre and the Irish National Theatre Society, *The Shadow of the Glen* is actually the first of Synge's plays to use irony as a principle of structure.[40] The whole play is based on what Nicholas Grene termed "the comic irony of the eavesdropper,"[41] i.e., a situation in which a man supposedly dead is listening to what goes on around him. Dramatic irony is

---

[39] *A Doll House* is indeed one of the most important intertexts of *The Shadow*. For an interesting comparison of Nora in the respective plays, and an analysis of Ibsen's influence on Synge, see McCormack, *Fool of the Family*, 160 and Ch. 10., and Murray, *Twentieth-Century Irish Drama*, 69-77. The objectionable nature of the link to Ibsen is noted also by Frazier, *Behind the Scenes*, 83.

[40] The phrase is, however, not to be understood in the New Critical sense as outlined by Cleanth Brooks in his article "Irony as a Principle of Structure," *Literary Opinion in America*, ed. M.D. Zabel (Gloucester, Mass.: Peter Smith, 1968) 729-41. It is intended to refer rather to the operation of the play in context.

[41] Nicholas Grene, "Synge's The Shadow of the Glen: Repetition and Allusion" (1974), *Critical Essays on John Millington Synge*, 81.

introduced quite early on, as the audience discovers that Dan is really alive, and watches the rest of the play with this knowledge in mind. It is from this tension that the play gains most of its dramatic impetus.

As noted above, the audience's expectations were clearly subverted by another obviously ironic moment: Nora walks out to a presumably better life on the road. In this scene, Synge sets up a pattern which repeats itself in his later plays: the standards of an enclosed community are disrupted by an intrusion from the outside (on this occasion, the Tramp), while it is revealed through the intruder how corrupt these standards in many ways are.[42]

The world of the tramp is undeniably presented as superior to the gloomy cottage in a remote glen with its grumbling, oppressive elderly man. In fact, Dan Burke, pretending to be dead in order to catch his wife misbehaving, is ironically shown to have been dead to all intents and purposes long before, as Nora talks about him as having been "always cold, every day since I knew him,—and every night" (35).[43] Although Nora's departure from a loveless marriage to the old scheming farmer has been interpreted by most later critics as her complete victory, the outcome still differs from Christy's situation in the final scene of *The Playboy of the Western World*. Gérard Leblanc, for instance, has pointed out that life with the tramp may certainly be livelier and emotionally richer; nonetheless, it is also harsh and far from comfortable. And Nora seems to be aware of this, since she responds to the Tramp's "[...] but it's fine songs you'll be hearing when the sun goes up, and there'll be no old fellow wheezing the like of a sick sheep close to your ear" by remarking that "I'm thinking it's myself will be

---

[42] James Pethica has pointed out that the dramatic pattern had a precedent in Douglas Hyde's *The Twisting of the Rope*, and also in *Cathleen ni Houlihan*. Pethica, "'A Young Man's Ghost,'" 8n27. Earlier non-Irish precedents of course abound.

[43] Gérard Leblanc, "Ironic Reversal as Theme and Technique in Synge's Shorter Comedies," *Aspects of the Irish Theatre*, eds. Patrick Rafroidi, Raymonde Popet and William Parker (Paris: Editions Universitaires, 1972) 53.

wheezing that time with lying down under the Heavens when the night is cold [...]" (57). When admiring the Tramp's poetic language and rhetorical skills, Leblanc reminds us we should not forget that *The Shadow of the Glen* also makes explicit "the *limits* of 'linguistic' salvation."[44]

The pattern of disruption by an outsider and the subsequent revelation of the community's flaws ends with an inevitable expulsion of the outsider, which again is a recurrent motif in a number of Synge's plays. Moreover, as in *The Playboy*, the community—here represented by Dan Burke and his wife's apparent lover Michael Dara—ultimately resort to 'peace over a drink' in an effort to heal the wounds inflicted by the intrusion. The final ironic moment[45] (ironic because of the preceding revelation of flaws) clearly works as a means of satire—which, of course, also holds true for the preference given to a life with a tramp over an accepted position within a (corrupt) society.

The Insight of Blindness: The Well of the Saints
In Synge's third play to be staged, *The Well of the Saints*, ironic moments create a positively more intricate pattern. From the relatively simple one-act plays the playwright has moved to complex texts with several layers of meaning which are hard to encompass within a single reading. In fact, the multifaceted nature of characters such as Martin and Mary Doul and the double-edged attitude of the villagers to them give rise to an immensely rich ironic interplay which is both humorous and tragic.

It may well be the complexity of the play's meaning that was responsible for its initial reception. *The Well of the Saints* was greeted with some negative feelings again: the Irish press was generally hostile, viewing the play as depicting squalor and

---

44 Leblanc, "Ironic Reversal," 54; my emphasis.
45 Cf. also Grene, "Synge's The Shadow of the Glen," 87.

sex.[46] Indifference and lack of interest prevailed shortly afterwards, and minimal audiences signified substantial losses for the Abbey Theatre.[47] It seems that even the most dogmatic nationalists chose to express their dislike of the author in the most convenient way, that is, by not going to the theatre. Nevertheless, reviews in the English press were positive, and an enthusiastic article about the play appeared in the Parisian journal *Revue de'l art dramatique*.[48] The article—written by Synge's friend, Henri Lebeau—brought Synge to the attention not only of French theatres but, by extension, also those in Germany and the Czech lands, and there were was soon a number of productions of the playwright's work in foreign language translations.

The play is remarkable for its satirical treatment of provincialism and close-mindedness and the way it sneers at a society governed by the concerns of one's own material wellbeing and by opportunistic deference to religion.[49] The chief irony in *The Well*, which to a large extent serves as a means of anti-provincial satire, is certainly the fact that the blind are shown to possess better insight than those who can see.[50]

A preceding part of this chapter demonstrated how easy it is to point out the ironic interplay between Synge's plays and the professed aims of what was later to become the Irish National

---

[46] A summary of the most important reviews may be found in McCormack, *Fool of the Family*, 281-82; and Dean, *Riot and Great Anger*, 76-77.

[47] Hunt, *The Abbey*, 62-63; Peter Kavanagh, *The Story of the Abbey Theatre* (New York: Devin-Adair, 1950) 50, quoted in Kiberd, *Synge and the Irish Language*, 243.

[48] McCormack, *Fool of the Family*, 282-83.

[49] As for the latter, the most obvious instance is provided by the scene where Martin Doul is mockingly dressed up in the Saint's cloak, while at the approach of the Saint the cloak is stripped off Martin in a rush, the onlookers grotesquely arrange themselves in veneration and immediately go quiet, as their only interest is to witness a miracle (85-89).

[50] The satirical intent seems also apparent in Synge's working title for the play which was "When the Blind See." Synge also called his gloomy, corrupt village Grianan, meaning "the sunny place" in Irish. McCormack, *Fool of the Family*, 276.

Theatre. And with *The Well of the Saints* one may wonder again about the nature of the "deeper thoughts and emotions" which supposedly reside in Martin and Mary Doul. It is true that Martin's language in particular is at times very elaborate and poetic—but in what context? Most notably, he employs his verbal skills to woo Timmy's designate wife and persuade her to run away with him (111-19). In another remarkable instance, he quite beautifully evokes a scene that features Timmy and Molly Byrne roasting in hell, while Martin pictures himself as a spectator who carefully withholds his delight from God's eyes (123). Even when Martin and Mary are read as tragic heroes for whom this world is too corrupt, their moral shortcomings can hardly be ignored.

More significant ironic moments are provided by Yeats's preface to the first edition of the play, published at the time of the premiere. Others have already focused on the myth established in that text, namely that Synge left for the Aran Islands immediately on Yeats's suggestion.[51] Nevertheless, another important statement is to be found in the preface, about which consensus by no means prevails: Yeats claims that the blind beggars are driven by a "dream of an impossibly noble life," while being "moved by no practical ambition," and that they are "so transformed" by the dream that they decide to revert to blindness.[52] In other words, according to Yeats there is a sharp contrast between the harsh reality of the world represented in the play and the ideal world of the beggars' noble dream.

Martin and Mary's dream requires closer examination but this has to be preceded by an important note: it would be rather insensitive to take Yeats's preface merely as the poet's personal interpretation of the play. One has to bear in mind the kind of

[51] Synge's diary records the date of the meeting as 21 December 1896, while Synge did not arrive on the Aran Islands until May 1898. McCormack, *Fool of the Family*, 140.

[52] W.B. Yeats, "Preface to the First Edition of The Well of the Saints," Synge, *Collected Works*, III.67.

negotiations concerning the approach of the Abbey Theatre at the time. Following the uproar surrounding the production of *The Shadow of the Glen*, and after the attack on that play had been renewed shortly before *The Well* was to open, Yeats expected another strongly negative reaction.[53] Hence, the preface should be read primarily as a defence, both of the play and the theatre itself. It is also true, however, that Yeats had always been adamant about his notion of Ireland as the realm of noble dreams, and in this respect his preface to *The Well* is certainly no exception. As we shall see, it is this very notion that is subject to multiple irony in the play.

The first thing that should be noted about the dream of the blind is that its nature goes through a series of significant changes in the play. Indeed, the word "dream" seems rather inappropriate for the entire Act I: it is mainly the talk of the villagers about Mary's fine skin and golden hair and Martin's good looks that makes them believe that they are "the finest man, and the finest woman, of the seven counties of the east" (73). The couple are in fact half-afraid of ever regaining their sight, since they seem to have a vague foreboding that it may all be just an *illusion* (72-74). Indeed, there is even a more immediate method of finding out the truth than having their eyes miraculously cured, namely, using their sense of touch, which is something they would never ever do. The illusion is rather pleasant, since not only can they believe in their own superior beauty, but they can also listen to the flattering voices of others forever, without having to do hardly any work. Their laziness often tends to be ignored, despite the fact that it is made manifest by several farcical scenes, particularly the opening of Act II which shows Martin idling and only very reluctantly cutting the sticks (103-7). The fact that the illusion is to a large extent the result of the villagers' macabre and acted flattery makes a substantial ironic comment on the alleged nobility of the "dream" the blind couple are supposed to maintain.

[53] See, for example, Saddlemyer, Introduction to Synge, *Collected Works*, III.xxiv.

When sight is given back to Martin and Mary, all the harshness and horror of this world is revealed. Nevertheless, stress is also placed on the essential superficiality of sight. Sight touches only the surface of things. Most of the conversation in the neighbourhood now concerns the appearance of the people, as Timmy disconcertedly remarks to Martin:

> But it's a queer thing the way yourself and Mary Doul are after setting every person in this place, and up beyond Rathvanna, talking of nothing, and thinking of nothing, but the way they do be looking in the face. [...] It's the devil's work you're after doing with your talk of fine looks, and I'd do right, maybe, to step in, and wash the blackness from my eyes. [111]

Although it was not actually Martin who had started the talk of fine looks, he had certainly spoken a lot on the subject. Despite this, he is the first to gain a deeper insight into people, as he proves in his subsequent speeches to Molly Byrne. He still praises Molly's good looks but stresses the particularity of his own perception of her, which he quotes as the reason why she should run away from the close-minded community with him: "come along with myself, for I'm seeing you this day, seeing you, maybe, the way no man has seen you in the world" (117). Again, it should not be forgotten that insight and eloquence seem to be the only way for a shabby old man to have any success with the most beautiful woman around, a fact which slightly qualifies the sublime nature of the world Martin describes to Molly.

In Act III, darkness falls on the couple again, and with it comes eventually the decision not to accept the cure any more. As I have noted, for Yeats—as indeed for many critics—this is a decision invoked by the ideal quality of their dream. There is no doubt that the reality of the village is too harsh for Martin and Mary to bear, while their disillusionment is limitless. The illusion they used to live in, on the other hand, surprisingly develops with the discovery of even more positive features. The beggars find out that golden hair, perfect skin and the looks of eternal youth can be replaced by long grey hair and a respectable beard, thus satisfying not only the requirements of passers-by but also their own desire for a comely appearance. The missing eyesight can be equally replaced by the senses of hearing and smell (129-33). This is why, on the approach of the Saint, they desperately try to escape from his cure, hiding behind a bush in a moment of bitter comedy antecedent of Beckett's Estragon attempting to hide behind the dry and almost leafless tree.[54]

Does this all imply, however, that the illusion they decide to live in is to be regarded as something transcendental and poetic? The way Martin and Mary describe their future world undoubtedly *is* lyrical:

> MARY DOUL: There's the sound of one of them twittering yellow birds do be coming in the spring-time from beyond the sea, and there'll be a fine warmth now in the sun, and a sweetness in the air, the way it'll be a grand thing to be sitting here quiet and easy, smelling the things growing up, and budding from the earth. [131]

Nevertheless, the reasons for their return to this fantasy are again multiple, one of them being their persistent reluctance to earn a living by work. Even the venerable grey beard is praised by Martin partially because "a priest itself would believe the lies of an old man would have a fine white beard growing on his chin" (131). Clearly, not only the inherent superiority of the illusion to the squalor of reality is crucial here. The reasons for choosing blindness are a careful balance of poetic dreaming on the one hand, and vanity and laziness on the other. The latter aspect then adds another ironic dimension to the play,

---

[54] Samuel Beckett, *The Complete Dramatic Works* (London: Faber, 1986) 69. Synge's influence on Beckett was explicitly acknowledged by the latter. See James Knowlson, *Damned to Fame: The Life of Samuel Beckett* (London: Bloomsbury, 1996) 57. A detailed critical discussion is to be found in James Knowlson and John Pilling, *Frescoes of the Skull: The Late Prose and Drama of Samuel Beckett* (London: Calder, 1979) 259-74.

Making Them Hop: The Playboy of the Western World

Synge's masterpiece, *The Playboy of the Western World*, is his most hilarious and at the same time most serious play, as it is also his most subversive and most complex. The plot, on the other hand, is again fairly simple: it is the story of a feeble young man who is running away from the law because he has killed his father. Arriving in a small village community, he is glorified as a mighty hero, until the moment when his supposedly dead father appears on the scene. The hero proceeds, under some pressure, to kill his father again, this time in front of the villagers. To his surprise, they turn against him, maintaining that "there's a great gap between a gallous story and a dirty deed" (169). However, Christy Mahon has by then been transformed into a strong individual who walks out of the door unabashed and victorious, followed by a subdued father. Here again, the pattern of a disruptive outsider repeats itself, one who demonstrates the community's blemishes, and his ultimate expulsion. Nevertheless, this time the stranger is clearly shown to have completely triumphed, conquering his oppressive father into the bargain and walking out with a smile on his face and a glorious story of folly to tell. The final moment of drawing the porter in order to let the metaphorical "bite" heal is thus all the more ironic.

The multifaceted nature of the central character can best be documented by the extreme diversity of readings that critics have produced over time. Many parallels have been drawn with Christy Mahon's fate. He has been interpreted variously as a Christ figure, a mock-Christ, a Cúchulainn, an Oedipus or a Charles Stuart Parnell. All these readings may maintain a degree of plausibility but each of them is far too one-sided. Declan Kiberd has in fact recently suggested that Christy may be viewed instead as mere empty space filled by the desires of the community, who project heroic qualities onto him. In this, Kiberd suggests, the Playboy is comparable to real Irish nineteenth-century Messianic heroes, from O'Connell to

Parnell, and the critics are quite similar to the Mayo community, each seeing in Christy their own desires.[62]

Yet, as Nicholas Grene correctly pointed out, the play should not be reduced to a literary interpretation of its central character. Grene claims that there are indeed several complementary sides to the play,[63] while none of them should be discarded for the sake of a coherent and/or savoury interpretation. But then again, Grene also admits that "it is hard to avoid stressing one side at the expense of another, difficult to find a critical view which will adequately represent the play's multiplicity."[64] In this sense, the play may indeed be "a work destined to be forever misinterpreted."[65]

Of all Synge's plays, *The Playboy* has the strongest farcical element to it. On the other hand, it is at the same time a kind of bildungsdrama,[66] dealing with the growth of its central character to maturity. These two levels are inextricably interwoven, as the growth of Christy follows a trajectory in which moments of glory alternate with ironic pitfalls.[67] Whenever the 'hero' seems to rise to new heights on the wings of his story, the pedestal is ironically snatched from under his feet: it may be a mere unexpected knock on the door which sends him whimpering behind Pegeen's back (85), or, more seriously, his dead father appears right after Christy lets the blow of the loy travel down to the old man's waist in his story

---

[62] Kiberd, *Inventing Ireland*, 180-81.

[63] Here Grene deliberately echoes Synge's own statement about the play. Cf. Nicholas Grene, "Approaches to The Playboy" (1975), *John Millington Synge's The Playboy*, 75.

[64] Grene, "Approaches to The Playboy," 75.

[65] Patricia Meyer Spacks, "The Making of The Playboy," *John Millington Synge's The Playboy*, 7.

[66] Bruce M. Bigley, "The Playboy as Antidrama" (1977), *John Millington Synge's The Playboy*, 98. Grene uses the expression "bildungsroman in little"; "Approaches to The Playboy," 82.

[67] Alan Price has poignantly likened this trajectory to a wave-like movement, consisting of "peaks" and "troughs," a device of dramatic contrast used frequently by, for example, Molière. Alan Price, "The Dramatic Imagination: The Playboy" (1961), *John Millington Synge's The Playboy*, 35.

[60]

(119). Indeed, farcical moments abound, ironically qualifying individual points of the hero's growth: when admiring his own face in a mirror, he is ambushed by the village girls and has to run and hide (95), while the celebration of his courage by the girls and the Widow Quin is terminated by Pegeen's unexpected appearance and her ensuing rage (105). Finally, in a moment of exquisite comedy, the 'serious,' poetic love scene between Christy and Pegeen is eventually completed by a Falstaffian blessing of Pegeen's father who is spectacularly drunk at the time, while immediately after the "Amen, O Lord!" in rushes Old Mahon and starts beating Christy (157).

While again irony works as a principle of the play's structure, it should be noted that the ironic moments merely shape the course of Christy's way to selfhood, while neither the comic, nor the serious are allowed to prevail. Or, in Grene's words, irony is made to operate in such a way that "Negative does not cancel out positive, but between the two an electric current is set flowing."[68] It is this spark of energy that creates the main driving force in the play, and at the same time complicates its meaning.

Christy may well be a kind of "mock-Christ who puts an end to crucifixion by killing the Father."[69] However, the audiences of the first production notoriously did not accept this notion by any means, and moved to kill the play in its turn. In fact, even the insurgency leader and revivalist intellectual Padraic Pearse—although initially an opponent of the play—later spoke of a metaphorical crucifixion in this context, claiming that "When a man like Synge [...] uses strange symbols which we do not understand, we cry out that he has blasphemed and we proceed to crucify him."[70]

[68] Grene, "Approaches to The Playboy," 78.
[69] Kenner, "The Living World of the Text," 118.
[70] Pádraic H. Pearse, *Collected Works of Pádraic H. Pearse: Political Writings and Speeches* (Dublin: Phoenix, 1924) 145.

The history of the greatest commotion in an Irish theatre has been well documented,[71] and there is again no reason to go into great detail here. Suffice it to say that when reading through the records of the first week's performances, one often has the sense that there were indeed two shows happening at the same time, while the one on the stage was often not the louder, or even the more comic.

There have been many analyses of the reasons for these disturbances, while most of them tended to treat the Abbey audience in a manner similar to Yeats and Lady Gregory, i.e., as a philistine mob. Whatever one may think of the attitudes of these people, collective or personal, it cannot be denied that they were, for the most part, a group of intelligent people, rather than a bunch of rowdies.[72] Their behaviour in the theatre, although not 'appropriate,' cannot be dismissed as mere hooliganism. Arguably, however, some politically motivated stubbornness was clearly in evidence: the audience insisted once more on treating the play as realistic. Interestingly enough, this applied not only to radical Catholic nationalists, but apparently also to many a unionist spectator (who saw *The Playboy* as a true, albeit appalling, depiction of the state of rural Ireland).[73]

The specific elements that contributed to the upheaval were again multiple. Clearly, several nationalist concepts were again mocked, including the Irish peasant or the chaste Irishwoman. Radical Catholic nationalists were also pricking their ears for offensive moments, as this was Synge, and, moreover, in what called itself the National Theatre. In fact, the evidence again suggests that the protest in the theatre was planned in advance.[74] However, the play in fact makes clever use of an

---

[71] Cf. Robert Hogan and James Kilroy, *The Abbey Theatre: The Years of Synge 1905-1909* (Dublin: The Dolmen Press, 1978) 123-62, or James Kilroy, *The "Playboy Riots"* (Dublin: Dolmen Press, 1971).

[72] Cf. Frazier, *Behind the Scenes*, 67-68, 214-17.

[73] Pilkington, *Theatre and the State*, 60-61.

[74] See McCormack, *Fool of the Family*, 319. Some hissing—allegedly also orchestrated beforehand—was heard, as a prelude to what was to come, during

effect which may prove uncomfortable to anyone seriously pondering the moral issues raised in the play, and not only a fervent turn-of-the-century patriot.

The first-night audience "broke up in disorder" at the use of the word "shift,"[75] a rather innocent expression for a woman's undergarment. Recent critics have, however, noted that this moment really amounted to a misplacement of anxieties, as immediately before the ill-famed expression was used, Christy had just killed his father in front of the villagers' eyes, thus transforming a tall tale of violence into a deed of blood.[76] The audience seemed to have happily accepted the fact that a parricide was made into a hero in the play. However, there was some discomfort at Old Mahon's first appearance with a bloody bandage on his head,[77] which ultimately culminated in an open protest after Christy proceeded to employ his loy once more, this time 'for real.'

Synge's actual strategy has been aptly summarised by Bruce Bigley: "through our responses to generic convention he forces us into uncomfortable moral positions; and through our conventional moral responses he keeps us from settling into comfortable aesthetic attitudes."[78] In other words, the violence of the reported initial killing is presented as part of a comic convention, and as such no-one is inclined to regard it as a moral issue. However, with the appearance of the father, real blood emerges onstage, the convention of the genre is

---

a revival of *The Shadow of the Glen* a week before the opening of *The Playboy*. McCormack, *Fool of the Family*, 302.

[75] Lady Gregory's telegram to Yeats. Quoted in Hogan and Kilroy, *The Abbey Theatre: The Years of Synge*, 126.

[76] Most prominently Grene in "Approaches to The Playboy," 87-88.

[77] Apparently, the detail of Mahon's injured head looked so realistic on the first night that the playwright Padraic Colum noted that the figure "with horribly-bloodied bandage upon his head" was "too representational." Quoted in Grene, "Approaches to The Playboy," 87. The naturalistic detail was avoided in later Abbey productions. The Widow Quin's admiring examination of Mahon's cleft skull may be added to Alan Price's list of moments that satirise the popular attraction of the "lurid." Cf. Price, "The Dramatic Imagination," 24.

[78] Bigley, "The Playboy as Antidrama," 90.

subverted and violence suddenly becomes manifest. Bigley is probably wrong about how disturbing this effect is to modern audiences, as when the play is seen for the first time the spectator hardly has enough time to ponder moral issues, the experience being chiefly one of bewilderment, or merely rather peculiar amusement (which is documented by the reception of the play by later audiences worldwide, who seemed to have viewed the play chiefly as a bizarre comedy). On the other hand, an audience specifically geared to issues like correct representation of a nation on the stage and hostile towards any attempt to satirise its moral standards was simply bound to be disturbed, not to say outraged. And if there were symbols which were not understood, to paraphrase Pearse once more, this seemed to have been only a marginal matter.

One of the greatest ironies remains that although *The Playboy* is certainly not mimetic in the sense of mirroring a particular socio-historical context in a realistic manner, the behaviour of the villagers in the play did in fact mirror the behaviour of the first-night audience: it was precisely at the moment when the community onstage turned against Christy that the audience turned against the play. And a further irony of the audience's reaction was noted by Kiberd: the people basically charged the stage shouting 'We are not a violent people!'[79]

In a letter to a friend, Synge considered writing a play about the worst kind of Irish country people, exclaiming "God, wouldn't they hop!"[80] It is hard to say whether the play he had in mind eventually became *The Playboy of the Western World*, a play which in an early draft had Christy elected county councillor by the dismal local community.[81] What is beyond doubt, however, is that many were indeed made to hop: virtually all the Dublin audience of the play. Synge could hardly have envisaged *such* a turmoil. The play certainly

---

[79] Kiberd, *Inventing Ireland*, 168.
[80] *The Collected Letters of John Millington Synge I*, ed. Ann Saddlemyer (Oxford: Clarendon Press, 1983) 116.
[81] McCormack, *Fool of the Family*, 229.

proved to be a tour de force as satire, offering the Irish nationalists a glimpse at themselves. Yet, the latter were far from adopting the implications of the unflattering reflection.

But there is a final paradox: very much like the earlier controversy over *The Countess Cathleen*, the 'Playboy Riots' provided the Abbey Theatre with a brilliant public relations campaign. This was already recorded in the course of the attacks on the theatre in the press, as one of the group's critics indignantly noted:

> The author of the play which has created such commotion in Dublin during the past few days could have hardly foreseen that his efforts would have obtained, unsolicited, such a huge advertisement. We are certain he did not seek it or desire it on the terms.[82]

True, Synge was in all probability not the kind of person to deliberately promote his work by raising violent controversy. Nevertheless, the uproar in its effect helped to establish the Irish National Theatre Society even more firmly as a focus of attention of both the press and the public in general. The fact that some of the theatre group left in reaction to the play proved to be a small price to pay in the long run.

Synge's "Vicious Bite"

It is perhaps characteristic of such situations that the early audiences who rejected Synge's satire also refused to discuss the objectionable plays as satirical at all. In this respect, the author of *The Playboy* makes an interesting comparison with his popular contemporary and also Abbey playwright William Boyle. Boyle was readily acknowledged as a satirist by the press and audiences alike. The chief reason for this is tellingly revealed in a quote from the *Irish Independent* review of Boyle's

---

[82] "The National Theatre," *The Irish Independent* 31 Jan. 1907: 4, quoted in Hogan and Kilroy, *The Abbey Theatre: The Years of Synge*, 140-41.

hit, *The Building Fund*: "it is satire, but it is satire that tickles rather than stings."[83] W.B. Yeats clearly shared the sentiment— but used it rather as an argument in defence of his fellow director, echoing in the same breath Swift's famous dictum on the subject: "Mr. Boyle['s] [...] satire is such as all men accept. [...] We have never doubted that what he assails is evil, and we are never afraid that it is ourselves." Conversely, "Mr. Synge [...] has discovered a new kind of sarcasm, and it is this sarcasm that keeps him, and may long keep him, from general popularity."[84] One suspects that Yeats would have been glad that Boyle's "tickling" satire has quietly petered out from the stage in Ireland as anywhere else, unlike Synge's blows of the loy. Nonetheless, when Synge expressed sincere hope in 1907 that if Ireland considered itself a healthy, living country, people should not "mind being laughed at without malice, as the people in every country have been laughed at in their comedies,"[85] he overestimated the level of tolerance pertaining to the current state of Ireland. The sensitive time of national emancipation allowed for his kind of humour and irony to be perceived solely as equivalent to Christy's "vicious bite."

The author of *The Playboy of the Western World* can, without a doubt, be viewed as an "ironic revolutionary," not exactly sharing the views of most nationalists but having a very clear social and anti-imperial agenda,[86] or indeed, more radically, as a writer striving for an artistic decolonisation of Ireland.[87] However, the double edge of his ironies is not to be ignored: Synge remains as much a writer with an ironic counter-revolutionary impulse. It was only gradually that he came to be accepted in Ireland with both of these strands acknowledged, finally "a likely gaffer in the end of all." In the meantime, Synge's international reputation grew steadily.

---

83 "Some Press Notices of Mr. Boyle's Plays," William Boyle, *The Building Fund: A Comedy in Three Acts* (Dublin and Waterford: M.H. Gill and Son, 1911) i.

84 W.B. Yeats, *Samhain: 1905*, reprinted in *Explorations*, 184.

85 J.M. Synge, Preface to *The Tinker's Wedding*, *Collected Works*, IV.3.

86 Murray, *Twentieth-Century Irish Drama*, Ch. 3, passim.

87 Kiberd, *Inventing Ireland*, Ch. 10, passim.

A curious entry in one of Synge's notebooks runs: "Man is not fashioned as are the swine and stars."[88] Essentially ambiguous and gracefully crafted, ironic and at the same time charged with a humanist impulse, the line sums up so much of Synge. It testifies, together with his succinct prefaces and miscellaneous notes on literature, to his ambition to create by means of the local a universally relevant poetic message. It also bears witness to another important strand in Synge: the tendency to pass moral judgement on the world, but typically through ironic and ambiguous statements whose music is often as important as the meaning of the words. The fact that he is justifiably regarded as a masterful precursor of European modernist drama and most of his plays continue to be staged throughout the world bears witness to the success of his universalist aspiration.

---

[88] Trinity College Dublin MS 4389 ff. 37-38. Quoted in McCormack, *Fool of the Family*, 124.

II. REJECTIONS

"Not a Theme for Poetry": Sean O'Casey and *The Silver Tassie*

The regrettable transformation of the Irish National Theatre from a challenging, controversial and often innovative stage into an authoritative, state-subsidised national institution in the late 1920s is best illustrated by focusing on important new dramas rejected by the Abbey directors and the reasons behind the individual rejections. Some of these plays were early efforts of talented young authors, while others were written by established playwrights, and with Sean O'Casey, by the current star of the Abbey repertoire itself. Although the context varied from case to case, there are a striking number of parallels. These in turn may serve as important indicators of both the National Theatre's politics and actual theatrical practice. Two plays in particular clearly demonstrate the ironic interaction between the alleged aims of the National Theatre and the way things really worked: Sean O'Casey's *The Silver Tassie* and Denis Johnston's *The Old Lady Says "No!"* At the same time, both of these works use irony as an essential means of dismantling the prevailing narratives of nationhood while also pioneering avant-garde techniques in the context of Irish drama of collective identity.

The rejection of these two plays was in fact preceded by the Abbey turning down several other important dramas. These earlier cases were arguably based on technical and/or material grounds, or on the fact that what was offered by the playwright went against the explicit objectives of the theatre. For instance, when the Abbey Directors decided to reject Joyce's play *Exiles* in 1917, Yeats wrote an apologetic letter to the author, giving the following explanation:

> We are a folk theatre, and now we have no longer any subsidy [...], we have had a hard struggle to live. The old days of subsidy enabled us to popularise after years of waiting a type of folk-drama, and that folk-drama now keeps the Theatre running. We can very seldom venture anything outside its range, and are chiefly experimental in one-act pieces which can be buoyed up by old favourites [...]. If we could give you a really fine performance we might venture it. But it is not possible to face at the same moment the limitations of players and of audience.[1]

After the withdrawal of Miss Annie Horniman's funding from the Abbey (1910), life became difficult for the theatre. Not only did it lack a playwright of Synge's genius, but it also had to be even more careful as to what type of plays it was staging. For the first time it needed to attract larger audiences merely to survive. Moreover, the lack of resources continued to influence the way the actors and other people involved in the productions were hired: there were almost no full-time employees in the theatre and most actors had to keep their regular jobs, which meant their time for rehearsals was severely restricted. This, combined with the lack of consistent actor training (a limitation universal in Ireland until very recently), could have turned a naturalist play with complex character psychology such as *Exiles* into a very poor show indeed. Yeats was being matter-of-fact with Joyce when he spoke of the "limitations of players."

What was of equal importance—but not mentioned by Yeats in his letter to Joyce—was the essential unwillingness of the

---

[1] W.B. Yeats to James Joyce, 8 Nov. 1917, quoted in *Theatre Business: The Correspondence of the First Abbey Theatre Directors*, ed. Ann Saddlemyer (University Park and London: Pennsylvania State University Press, 1982) 15.

Directorate to produce "modern drama of society."[2] The Abbey eventually came to stage the occasional Strindberg but it was only in 1923 when Ibsen was first produced (*A Doll's House*), while world drama never really became a major strand at the Abbey.[3] The only notable exception in terms of other dramatic genres were the plays of G.B. Shaw: first, there was the audacious production of *The Shewing-up of Blanco Posnet* in 1909, which was however motivated to a large extent by the need to re-confirm nationalist credentials harmed by the performance of Synge's *Playboy* and other controversial plays, rather than by any sense that there was a need for a greater variety of genres.[4] In 1916-17, the Abbey presented an entire season of Shaw, comprising six plays in total, including *John Bull's Other Island*, written for the Abbey over twelve years previously but still not produced there at the time due to its technical requirements (the play features an onstage car accident) and the lack of suitable actors, particularly for the role of the Englishman Broadbent.[5]

---

[2] W.B. Yeats, *Samhain: 1902*, reprinted in Yeats, *Explorations*, 95-97.

[3] This was initially also due to the conditions under which the theatre's patent had been issued, while later it was solely down to the insistence of the Directorate on staging mainly plays by Irish authors. In order to produce world drama, the Dublin Drama League was founded by Abbey director Lennox Robinson (1918). It featured many other directors as well as actors of the Abbey, and eventually evolved into the professional Gate Theatre (1929). Cf. Hunt, *The Abbey*, 114-15.

[4] See *Shaw, Lady Gregory and the Abbey: A Correspondence an a Record*, eds. Dan H. Laurence and Nicholas Grene (Gerrards Cross: Colin Smythe, 1993) xiv-xv.

[5] Laurence and Grene, *Shaw, Lady Gregory and the Abbey*, xi. The play became one of the most successful pieces in the National Theatre's repertoire, revived every year until 1931 (xxii). The Abbey eventually also staged Shaw's satirical recruitment play, *O'Flaherty, V.C.* (1920). However, the original production was postponed in 1915 due to fears of controversy with Dublin Castle and the British military authorities, and the fact that potentially undermining the recruitment campaign for WWI was perceived as a greater problem than aggravating radical nationalists. Cf. R.F. Foster, *W.B. Yeats: A Life. II. The Arch-Poet* (Oxford and New York: Oxford University Press, 2003) 29; Pilkington, *Theatre and the State*, 77.

The plays staged by the theatre after the death of Synge were mainly popular comedies, bland realist pieces or revivals of previous productions. Those supposedly in the know used to joke that new plays were tested by the Directors for a mysterious "P.Q.," i.e., "peasant quality."[6] Thus, it is hardly surprising that the modern, urban-based *Exiles* was rejected. Yeats was probably right in thinking that a standard Abbey audience would not be impressed by Joyce's concerns in the play, and that the theatre would not be able to give the play an adequate production; but also the play did not fit the 'Abbey style' of predominantly rural kitchen plays (termed "folk-drama" by Yeats).

However, adherence to the Abbey style, together with the lack of new talent and resources in fact meant that "[b]y 1918 both players and playwrights had reached a point where repetition and insularity were seriously stifling creative work," to quote an Abbey historian.[7] The striking success of the theatre on its English tours also became a thing of the past, as by the early 1910s the Abbey plays would have been considered dated due to the rise of modernism on the English stage.[8] The alarming material situation of the National Theatre Society—which had to mortgage its buildings in June 1923 to clear an overdraft of £2,000[9]—was slightly alleviated by the state subsidy granted in 1925. Nevertheless, it was only the arrival of Sean O'Casey that really saved the theatre from bankruptcy.[10]

In his three 'Dublin plays,' *The Shadow of the Gunman* (1923), *Juno and the Paycock* (1924) and *The Plough and the Stars* (1926), O'Casey gave the Abbey some of its most popular plays ever.[11] Changing the stereotypical rural setting into one of urban

---

6   Cf. Kiberd, *Inventing Ireland*, 220.
7   Hunt, *The Abbey*, 115.
8   Flannery, *W.B. Yeats and the Idea of a Theatre*, 346.
9   Foster, *W.B. Yeats: A Life*, II.236.
10   Hunt, *The Abbey*, 134. Lionel Pilkington has recently discussed at length the importance of O'Casey's plays and their politics even for the state subsidy to be granted to the Abbey. Pilkington, *Theatre and the State*, 95-99.
11   See, for instance, Foster, *W.B. Yeats: A Life*, II.258-59.

slums, O'Casey set about revising the ideologies that were involved in the struggle for an independent Irish state. The plays dramatise the three violent conflicts of the beginning of the century—the Civil War, the War of Independence and the Easter Rising respectively—viewing these events from the perspective of the Dublin poor and focusing on a critique of the nationalist idea of heroism.

The instant popularity of O'Casey's tragicomedies may indeed seem surprising, as all of them offered radical reconsiderations of recent events experienced by most Dubliners at first hand, while at the same time challenging particular views that would have still been held by many in the audience. Indeed, an open protest was staged on the fourth night of *The Plough and the Stars*. It was organised chiefly by the widows of leaders or prominent victims of the Easter Rising (including Hanna Sheehy-Skeffington and Mrs Patrick Pearse) whose indignation over the debunking of their husbands' convictions was more than understandable. Yeats made another speech in defence of the play and the freedom of the arts (taking care, as with the *Playboy*,[12] to hand it over to the press beforehand), protesters were again removed by the police, but this time the play continued to run for the rest of the week unhindered and to full houses. A prolonged battle over *The Plough and the Stars* ensued in the press, the most prominent voices being Mrs Sheehy-Skeffington and the author, while the play had already been attacked by the writers Liam O'Flaherty, Brinsley MacNamara and Austin Clarke. Similarly to the controversies over Synge's work, however, the protest and the following debate ultimately brought O'Casey's name to the attention of the public throughout Ireland and England, as well as in America. In the end, the protesters again managed to achieve rather the opposite of what they had intended.[13]

---

[12] Dean, *Riot and Great Anger*, 81.

[13] For a more detailed account of the controversy, see Hunt, *The Abbey*, 124-30, or Foster, *W.B. Yeats: A Life*, II.305-307. An amusing version of the 'riot' was provided by playwright and O'Casey's friend Denis Johnston in a

O'Casey's 'Dublin plays,' particularly *The Plough and the Stars*, soon became national classics, despite their open critique of the social conditions pertaining in Dublin on the one hand, and of nationalist ideologies on the other. The reasons for this ironic change of attitude towards the plays were multiple. One very important factor was that the setting of the plays, depicting the desperate situation in Dublin tenements, proved to be distant enough to the audience. The living conditions of the Dublin poor were certainly to be pitied but they were not of direct concern to most audience members, who in fact mainly represented the elite of the new state.[14] For these people, the tenements were more or less a detached, alien world. As for the poor themselves, they could for the most part hardly afford to go to the theatre.

Moreover, O'Casey "could be touted as a plebeian genius, given a welcome which was a testimony to the wonderful tolerance of the ruling order," to use Declan Kiberd's words,[15] despite the fact that O'Casey's image as a working-class playwright was largely stylised.[16] Kiberd was also right in claiming that, in his early plays, O'Casey runs a dangerous line between providing popular entertainment and questioning the audience's assumptions, while this technique may have the effect that "people, confronted with a sweetened propaganda pill, might learn how to suck off the sugar coating and leave the pill behind."[17] O'Casey's critique of ideas and ideologies needs in itself to be viewed in context: it centres predominantly on Republican ideology, and as such would have been very much

contemporary newspaper and a later Thomas Davis lecture: see Denis Johnston, "Sean O'Casey: An Appreciation," *Daily Telegraph* 11 Mar. 1926, reprinted in *Sean O'Casey: Modern Judgments*, ed. Ronald Ayling (London: Macmillan, 1969) 82-83, and Denis Johnston, "O'Casey in the Twenties," *The O'Casey Enigma*, ed. Micheál Ó hAodha (Cork and Dublin: Mercier Press, 1980) 24-26.

14 Kiberd, *Inventing Ireland*, 233.
15 Kiberd, *Inventing Ireland*, 233.
16 See, for instance, Nicholas Grene, *The Politics of Irish Drama. Plays in Context from Boucicault to Friel* (Cambridge: Cambridge University Press, 1999) 119.
17 Kiberd, *Inventing Ireland*, 221.

in tune with the politics of the contemporaneous Cumann na nGaedheal government and the social elite of the Free State.[18]

O'Casey need not be accused, however, of complicity with the new political regime, as he in fact demolishes *any* worldview presented by individual characters in the three plays, including even the Covey's socialist ideas in *The Plough*, by ridiculing them as vain speechifying that goes hand-in-hand with cowardice and an essential unwillingness to act. What is left standing are only the actions of pragmatic, good-hearted women; nevertheless, these take place in hopelessly tragic circumstances: the women have nowhere to move on to. This, in its effect, is not satire any more, as every available view is mocked, while the impulse for improvement lacks any direction. The audience is left with the ultimate tragic feeling that "th' whole worl's in a terrible state o' chassis"; despite the fact that the final tragedy is more than balanced by the comedy provided by some hilarious slum figures with a colourful idiom (described by Denis Johnston succinctly as delivering "a series of word-poems in dialect").[19] There is certainly a powerful mixture of emotions but hardly one that could offend, or more radically, move people to change. Clear impulses for social and political action tend to be communicated only in O'Casey's later drama. However, with the exception of *The Silver Tassie*, the extravagant *Cock-a-doodle Dandy*, and a few one-acts, this has in turn brought his work close to open agit-prop, making the artistic quality suffer severely.

---

[18] Cf. Pilkington, *Theatre and the State*, 95-96.

[19] Johnston, "Sean O'Casey: An Appreciation," 85. Kiberd is perhaps too harsh in calling O'Casey's early characters "urban leprechauns and sloganeering caricatures." However, some prominent characters really *are* caricatured: take Joxer Daly, Uncle Peter or Fluther, for instance. Cf. Kiberd, *Inventing Ireland*, 232. Christopher Murray, on the other hand, offers an interesting analysis of the juxtaposition of "chassis" with comedy in *Juno and the Paycock*; in contrast to the present essay, he sees the final cathartic laughter as reinforcement of the audience's sense of responsibility. Cf. Murray, *Twentieth-Century Irish Drama*, 103-4.

When writing his next play after *The Plough*— *The Silver Tassie*—which was to dramatise World War I and the attitudes of the Irish towards it, O'Casey decided that

> There was no importance in trying to do the same thing again, letting the second play imitate the first, and the third the second. He wanted a change from what the Irish critics had called burlesque, photographic realism, or slices of life, though the manner and method of two of the plays were as realistic as the scents stealing from a gaudy bunch of blossoms.[20]

And indeed, although the first act of *The Silver Tassie* has been taken by most critics as running in the same vein as the earlier plays (Yeats even claimed that it was the best first act that O'Casey had ever written),[21] it rather parodies the early O'Casey, especially in moments like the exaggerated farce of Sylvester and Mrs. Foran crawling under the bed (35)[22] or the synchronised tapping of Simon and Sylvester with their pipes (27). At the same time, the setting features a number of symbolic objects as the easel with a photograph of the heroic footballer in a silver frame, the purple shield with silver medals, placed on an altar-like gleaming stand, the gun which is being conspicuously polished by Susie Monican (21-22), and eventually the silver tassie itself (38-39).

However, it is the second act that marks the greatest departure from the style of the preceding plays. The war is staged in a powerful expressionist manner, with no gunfire to be heard and only flashes of light to be seen (67), while the nameless soldiers comment on their experience through ritualised chanting, which eventually culminates in an ironic religious celebration of the Gun and God (64-67). The soldiers' chant is moreover presided over by the terrifying allegorical

---

20 Sean O'Casey, *Rose and Crown* (New York: Macmillan, 1956) 32.
21 W.B. Yeats to Sean O'Casey, 20 Apr. 1928, quoted in Foster, *W.B. Yeats: A Life*, II.367.
22 Page references in brackets are to Sean O'Casey, *Three More Plays* (London: Macmillan/ New York: St Martin's Press, 1969).

figure of the Croucher whose identity seems to oscillate between a biblical prophet, a death-figure and a common soldier.

Acts III and IV return to the combination of the realist and the symbolic seen in the first act. In Act III, the absence of acknowledgement given to the returned soldiers is indicated by the continuation of their non-identity from the previous act, since in the hospital they exist yet again only as numbers.[23] The fourth act, finally, focuses on the ultimate erasure of the crippled soldiers from other people's lives. The image of Harry is emblematic of the fate of many: the heroic footballer and winner of the silver cup presented in Act I turns into a helpless figure in a wheelchair, with the likewise mangled silver trophy in his hands, while others are gracefully and carelessly waltzing in the ballroom (105-6). The final juxtaposition of lush life — which also includes the blossoming nature outside the windows — with the maimed and frustrated war hero is double-edged, however. Susie parts from Harry asserting that the crippled young soldiers:

> have gone to live their own way in another world. Neither I nor you [Jessie] can lift them out of it. [...] We can't give sight to the blind or make the lame walk. We would if we could. It is the misfortune of war. As long as wars are waged, we shall be vexed by woe; strong legs shall be made useless and bright eyes made dark. But we, who have come through the fire unharmed, must go on living. [105-6]

In the same way as the adjacent merry dance, Susie's claim is both a statement of brutal fact (the wounds cannot be undone and the unafflicted have to go on living) and at the same time serves as a powerful demonstration of the society's hypocrisy: it was the society, including Susie, who sent the young men to war and benefited from their involvement, and who now refuses to associate itself with them. The concluding remark by

[23] Cf. also Kiberd, *Inventing Ireland*, 242 and n9.

Mrs. Foran ultimately provides an ironic emphasis on the dark side of Susie's assertion: "It's a terrible pity Harry was too weak to stay an' sing his song, for there's nothing I love more than the ukulele's tinkle, tinkle in the night-time" (106).[24] Irony, and particularly ironic treatment of history, may indeed be seen to define the tone of The Silver Tassie throughout.[25]

O'Casey's audacious attempt to employ avant-garde influences in his dramatisation of the Great War resulted in what became probably the most publicised rejection by the Abbey Theatre. Yeats disliked The Silver Tassie profoundly, while Lady Gregory and fellow Abbey director Lennox Robinson also had reservations (albeit not to the extent that this would prevent the play from being produced).[26] It was Yeats alone, however—fated to mutual misunderstanding with O'Casey, as Roy Foster puts it[27]—who immediately dispatched a rejection letter. O'Casey, incensed by Yeats's comments on the play and the way the most successful Abbey playwright was being treated by the condescending arch-poet, decided to publish his correspondence with the Abbey directorate in The Observer (3 June 1928). This led to a series of public invectives from both sides, and hostilities were only reluctantly laid to rest.[28]

Yeats complained in his letter to O'Casey that the play lacked a subject, a central character, "psychological unity [and] the unity of action." Moreover, what seemed to him seriously amiss was that the author was not writing from personal

---

24 Heinz Kosok speaks of an "authorial irony [as] an indictment of th[e] lack of comprehension" on the part of the soldiers' families and friends. Heinz Kosok, "Two Irish Perspectives on World War I: Bernard Shaw and Sean O'Casey," Hungarian Journal of English and American Studies 2.2 (1996): 23-24.

25 Christopher Murray, Seán O'Casey: Writer at Work (Dublin: Gill and Macmillan, 2004) 192.

26 Murray, Seán O'Casey, 201.

27 Foster, W.B. Yeats: A Life, II.259.

28 For a detailed account of the conflict, see Foster, W.B. Yeats: A Life, II.366-372 and Murray, Seán O'Casey, 200-205.

experience.[29] Many critics have pointed out that the former Aristotelian claim would have clearly disqualified O'Casey's earlier plays as well, together with many other Abbey standards, while the latter actually put in question even Yeats's own drama, a fact that O'Casey indignantly spelled out in his reply.[30] Besides, O'Casey had two brothers and a brother-in-law who served in the British Army during the war and took a great interest in the personal experience of returning soldiers, to such an extent that the director of the eventual first production of the play in London was amazed at how much the civilian O'Casey knew about warfare and life in the trenches.[31] To put it briefly, Yeats may have been right in thinking the play "laborious"[32] but his objections were misphrased, to say the least.

There were clearly other, unacknowledged reasons for Yeats's brusque refusal of *The Silver Tassie*. Apart from the simple fact that the poet did not like it—which is not as trivial a statement as it may appear, since as noted in the preceding discussion of Yeats, he was very much a self-appointed high judge of art—there were other implicit reasons similar to those behind the rejection of Joyce's *Exiles*. *The Silver Tassie* was clearly not a play in the Abbey style, while both its methods and theme were not considered relevant to the national theatre's concern. Moreover, again problems with providing an adequate production for the play were clearly to be envisaged, due to the essential lack of theatrical resources noted above, and the general unwillingness of the Abbey to experiment.

In addition to the obvious mismatch with the accepted Abbey formula, Yeats's attitude to the thematic of *The Silver Tassie* played a significant role. Yeats was opposed to war as a subject for art. Despite the fact that he saw no problem in becoming involved with the armed insurrection at home in his

---

[29] W.B. Yeats to Sean O'Casey, 20 Apr. 1928, quoted in Foster, *W.B. Yeats: A Life*, II.367-68.

[30] Kosok, "Two Irish Perspectives on World War I," 22; Kiberd, *Inventing Ireland*, 240-41 and n3.

[31] Grene, *The Politics of Irish Drama*, 244; Murray, *Seán O'Casey*, 208.

[32] Yeats to O'Casey, 20 Apr. 1928, 368.

own poems like "Easter 1916,"[33] he maintained to the very end of his life that the Great War with its "passive suffering" was "not a theme for poetry";[34] here, the lack of heroes standing out in the mass slaughter may have been Yeats's chief objection[35] as an artist who adored individual achievement throughout his entire career. However, apart from its essential anti-war message, *The Silver Tassie* criticises also the lack of acknowledgement of Irish involvement in World War I. The play summarises its attitude to this national exclusion in a satirical micro-image in Act IV where a telephone incessantly rings while Simon, Sylvester and Mrs. Foran are very reluctant to answer it. When they eventually do so, they can hear only "buzzing and a roaring noise," cannot get the message and decide to put it down and pretend that it never rang (90-93). The nationalist refusal to honour the involvement of their compatriots, many of whom shared their own loyalty to the cause of Irish freedom, in the Great War was eventually to evolve into an almost general amnesia for decades to come, both in the official approach to the matter, and also in nationalist history writing.[36] It may well have been that this particular propensity to quickly forget on the part of the population which still made up a large section of the Abbey audience only contributed to Yeats's dismissal of a play that already went very much against his artistic grain.

Over the years, most critics have been far from discounting *The Silver Tassie* in a manner similar to Yeats. Declan Kiberd however remains fairly unique in claiming that the play is "the writer's most accomplished play" and maintains "a near-miraculous balance between the real and the symbolic."[37] The

---

33 Cf. Kiberd, *Inventing Ireland*, 246.

34 W.B. Yeats, Introduction to *The Oxford Book of Modern Verse 1892-1935* (Oxford: Clarendon Press, 1936) xxxiv. This was also Yeats's justification for his notorious omission of Siegfried Sassoon, Wilfred Owen and other important war poets from the anthology.

35 Grene, *The Politics of Irish Drama*, 243-44.

36 Declan Kiberd discusses the issue in his *Inventing Ireland*, 239-40.

37 Kiberd, *Inventing Ireland*, 241, 240.

majority of the reviewers of the first production (at the Apollo Theatre, London, October 1929) regarded the play as a challenging, although rather chaotic piece of drama that would clearly never be a popular success.[38] *The Times* critic Charles Morgan called it "almost a masterpiece" but made in his otherwise mostly positive assessment the following poignant observation: the play "fails sometimes with a great tumbling failure."[39] *The Silver Tassie* is simply too unbalanced in terms of style, as the contrast between the second act and the rest of the play is rather too stark. It is very much a director's play[40] and, quite possibly, an inspired director, teamed up with outstanding stage and lighting designers, would be able to create an exciting production of the play, one that would in all likelihood suppress the realistic element somewhat, stressing the symbolic signs that provide a line of continuity between individual acts, and, of course, place the musical aspects of the play in the foreground. As a matter of fact, *The Silver Tassie* has recently been produced as an opera, and Foster may be correct in observing that this genre is "perhaps its natural destination."[41]

What is certain, however, is that the rejection of *The Silver Tassie* deprived the Abbey of one of its greatest playwrights ever, leaving it back in the realms of insipid realism and derivative comedy for several decades. O'Casey's career with the theatre began with popularity ironically achieved through criticising its audiences' beliefs, while, unlike with Synge, general esteem for the playwright was an instant matter. Nevertheless, being eventually criticised for too much innovation and for using topics allegedly inappropriate to the

---

[38] For a summary of the reviews, see Murray, *Seán O'Casey*, 208.

[39] *The Times*, 12 Oct. 1929, quoted in Brendan Kennelly, Introduction to *Landmarks of Irish Drama* (London: Methuen, 1988) 268-69.

[40] Hugh Hunt discusses some problems of direction and design posed by the play in *The Abbey*, 131.

[41] Foster, *W.B. Yeats: A Life*, II.367. The opera version by Mark Antony Turnage was premiered by the English National Opera in 2000. Murray, *Seán O'Casey*, 484n64.

Abbey, his decision to remain working in England turned into a permanent one.

"Up the Living Departed!" Denis Johnston's *The Old Lady Says "No!"*

The Old Lady Says "No!" (1929), a "Romantic Play in Two Parts with Choral Interludes" written by the young Denis Johnston was rejected by the Abbey Theatre in 1928. Some of the reasons for the rejection were similar to the case of *The Silver Tassie*: the play obviously did not fit the Abbey style, and probably would not be given a suitable production at the theatre, while some of its concerns must have been perceived as too subversive for the theatre's good, particularly its targeting of both Republican nationalism and the Free State elite.[1]

However, Yeats was well aware that he was dealing with a promising new playwright, and as the Abbey was sorely in need of such, went through Johnston's original manuscript with great care, suggesting changes and virtually rewriting whole passages.[2] Somewhat annoyed by this, Johnston did the opposite to what the Abbey Director proposed when reworking the play, making it even more radically subversive; and, to be fair to Yeats, he did admit that the second version of the play

---

[1] For a discussion of the play as a political attack, see Pilkington, *Theatre and the State*, 105-6.

[2] For a detailed account of Yeats's revision see Denis Johnston, *Orders and Desecrations: The Life of the Playwright Denis Johnston*, ed. Rory Johnston (Dublin: Lilliput Press, 1992) 59-60, and Harold Ferrar, *Denis Johnston's Irish Theatre* (Dublin: The Dolmen Press, 1973) 25-26. It is interesting to note that Yeats apparently did not tackle any of the parodic moments concerning *Cathleen ni Houlihan*, although the specific allusions to his and Lady Gregory's play were extremely clear.

was a much better piece of drama, although he was still unwilling to have it staged at the national theatre. As he did not want to lose the playwright, though, he offered a small subsidy for the play to be performed at the Peacock by the Drama League.[3]

The rejection of the play has traditionally been connected with the name of Lady Gregory rather than Yeats, mainly due to the legendary story that the author himself propounded about the event. In a preface to the play, entitled "Opus One," Johnston claimed that the manuscript which originally bore the name "Shadowdance" came back to him from the Abbey with an attached inscription "The old lady says No!," the implication being that the old lady in question was Lady Gregory. The inscription was then deliberately interpreted as a suggestion for a new title, and immediately adopted.[4]

Despite the fact that Lady Gregory was certainly not happy about the play, calling it "impossible" in her diaries,[5] the details of her role in the rejection remain unclear, while there is some evidence that Johnston (co-)fabricated the story,[6] as such a procedure would have been quite in tune with the play's method and tone. What is more important, however, is that the title clearly refers not so much to Lady Gregory but to the allegorical Shan Van Vocht/Cathleen ni Houlihan of nationalist mythology, an icon appearing in the play as one of the central characters. At the same time, the nature of the title as a mere remark which, at least at first glance, bears a rather cryptic relation to the play's action reflects very well both its style and method of creation as a partially devised piece.

The Old Lady Says "No!" is a work of high modernism *par excellence*: it is full of quotations, borrowings and allusions, proceeds by a free association of ideas in the mind of the central

3 Johnston, *Orders and Desecrations*, 59-60.
4 Denis Johnston, "Opus One," *Selected Plays of Denis Johnston*, ed. Joseph Ronsley (Gerrards Cross: Colin Smythe, 1983) 20.
5 Quoted in Murray, *Twentieth-Century Irish Drama*, 121.
6 Nicholas Grene, "Modern Irish Literary Manuscripts," *Treasures of the Library Trinity College Dublin*, ed. Peter Fox (Dublin: Royal Irish Academy, 1986) 230-38.

character, and typically confronts various notions of time, as the main part of the action takes place within a few historical seconds. The body of the play consists in an extended play-within-the-play framed by an initial dramatic situation in which a pompous, sentimental dramatic piece is performed about the heroic Robert Emmet and his notorious 1803 rising. This opening melodrama, the text of which is a brilliant collage chiefly of fiery nineteenth-century patriotic verse,[7] is abruptly terminated when the main actor gets accidentally knocked out by an awkward colleague. A doctor is called in from the audience, and while he is looking for a rug to cover the legs of the unconscious star, the audience is transported into the mind of the actor, experiencing his hallucination.

The context of a dream enabled Johnston to discard causality and logic in favour of a free blending of images, situations and even individual characters. In relation to this, a debate ensued at quite an early stage over whether the play should be labelled "expressionist." Johnston himself took part in the debate by admitting to some inspiration from watching expressionist plays (particularly George S. Kaufman and Marc Connelly's *Beggar on Horseback* and the *The Land of Many Names* by Czech painter and writer Josef Čapek) but denied that *The Old Lady* was expressionist drama,[8] perhaps chiefly because of the association of the term with the humourless political plays of German practitioners of the method, Georg Kaiser and Ernst Toller. The mutual difference has been accurately summarised by D.E.S. Maxwell: Johnston's play is far from expressing the

---

[7] The material used in the Emmet melodrama has been partially acknowledged by the author (in "Opus One" and "A Note on What Happened"). Most of it was specifically identified by Curtis Canfield in his *Plays of Changing Ireland* (New York: Macmillan, 1936); Canfield's list is reprinted in *Selected Plays of Denis Johnston*, 87-89. Additional identification was made by Christine St. Peter in her annotated edition of the play; see Denis Johnston, *The Old Lady Says "No!"* ed. Christine St. Peter (Washington, D.C.: The Catholic University of America Press/ Gerrards Cross: Colin Smythe, 1992) 57-62.

[8] Johnston, "Opus One," 22; Denis Johnston, "A Note on What Happened," *Selected Plays of Denis Johnston*, 83.

existential worries of its German counterparts, and instead uses "comic deflation."[9] Indeed, *The Old Lady* is for the most part astonishingly hilarious. The other basic point of difference, as Maxwell pointed out, is that Johnston, contrary to the German authors, localises his action specifically into contemporary Dublin.[10]

The inspiration by the expressionists is on the other hand quite apparent in the way Johnston uses the sole consciousness of the dreamer as the play's only unifying factor, while also adopting the structure of the dreamer's quest.[11] From the perspective of theatrical practice, the set and lighting effects are also employed in an expressionist manner, constituting an organic flow of intermingling scenes and motifs, and the same can certainly be said about the role-doubling.[12] Most importantly, language in the play often works merely as material for music, while meaning is partially subordinated to rhythm and orchestration (the most remarkable instance being the passage in which the Speaker, the General, O'Cooney, and eventually several other characters speak/sing at the same time).[13] All this makes *The Old Lady* the first, and probably the greatest, Irish avant-garde comedy.

Any discussion of influences needs to highlight the presence of Joyce's *Ulysses* behind *The Old Lady*.[14] The affinity concerns

---

9 D.E.S. Maxwell, "Waiting for Emmet," *Denis Johnston: A Retrospective*, ed. Joseph Ronsley (Gerrards Cross: Colin Smythe, 1981) 30-31.

10 D.E.S. Maxwell, *A Critical History of Modern Irish Drama 1891-1980* (Cambridge: Cambridge University Press, 1984) 118.

11 Grene, *The Politics of Irish Drama*, 154-55.

12 For a further analysis of expressionist techniques utilised in the play, see Curtis Canfield, "A Note on the Nature of Expressionism and Denis Johnston's Plays," *Denis Johnston: A Retrospective*, 38-48.

13 Johnston has indeed claimed that the intention of the group was to see "whether the emotional appeal of music could be made use of in terms of theatrical prose, and an opera constructed that did not have to be sung." "Opus One," 20.

14 Cf. Joseph Ronsley, Introduction to *Selected Plays of Denis Johnston*, 12. Nicholas Grene speaks about *The Old Lady* as a theatrical equivalent to *Ulysses*. *The Politics of Irish Drama*, 152.

primarily the use of techniques such as stream of consciousness (as mentioned above), the use of language and characters, and the mixing of genres. A rather far-fetched parallel has even been made with *Finnegans Wake*—which Johnston decided to comment upon later[15]—but there seems to be only one, albeit quite interesting point of contact: in contrast to the *Wake*, the main body of the play takes place *within* a split sentence, whose final part ultimately seals its rambling structure.

Johnston also extensively employs, and frequently parodies, the work of some of his immediate predecessors or contemporaries, perhaps even more so than Joyce. Consider for instance the character of the Blind Man: his diction is recognisably Syngean,[16] while his noble ancestry and special abilities betray something of Yeats's character of the blind, noble poet Raftery: "Why should you not take my arm, stranger, for I'm telling you, my fathers are Kings in Thomond so they are" (65);[17] "I do have to laugh sometimes and I hearing the wings of the Queer Ones beating under the arch of the sky." (66) Johnston's visionary is indeed somewhat cynical as well, which in turn aligns him with Yeats's Blind Man in his drama *On Baile's Strand*. The oracular capacity of the Blind Man obviously follows a long tradition dating back at least to Greek antiquity, although it appears in the play with a specifically Irish inflection which concerns the power of the militant dead over the living:

> It takes a dark man to see the will-o'-the-wisps and the ghosts of the dead and the half dead and them that will never die while they can find lazy, idle hearts ready to keep their venom warm. [67]

---

15 Johnston admits to the use of one specific expression which appears in *Finnegans Wake* but dismisses any further affinities. Cf. Johnston, "Opus One," 22.

16 Grene, *The Politics of Irish Drama*, 153.

17 Page references in brackets are to *Selected Plays of Denis Johnston*.

The unusual insight into the community that the Blind Man possesses makes him closely resemble Martin Doul in Synge's *The Well of the Saints*: "Oh, but it is not myself that is dark at all, but them—blind and drunk with the brave sight of their own eyes." However, at the same time this insight moves very close to parody:

> For why would they care that the winds is cold and the beds is hard and the sewers do be stinking and steaming under the stone sets of the streets, when they can see a bit of rag floating in the wild wind, and they dancing their bloody Ceilidhes over the lip of Hell! [67]

The visionary's apocalyptic presence is also ultimately qualified by his grotesque role in the final dance of the Shadows. Mounting a chair, the blind man proclaims: "The shadows are gathering, gathering. They're coming to dance at a wake. An' I playing for them on the gut box" (75). In fact, the dual nature of the blind seer is already announced early on in his encounter with the Speaker: "walk with me and I'll put you on your way" (65). Here, Johnston's exquisite pun refers both to a visionary whose advice is to be followed, and at the same time to the "blind leading the blind."

Another major presence in *The Old Lady* is the playwright's friend O'Casey. The whole tenement scene in Part Two represents a pastiche of his Dublin plays (while a caricature of O'Casey himself appears in the play as the cap-wearing playwright O'Cooney),[18] which begins with its very setting and culminates in the travesty of an O'Casey dying scene,[19] while the atmosphere of a brothel is taken from the Nighttown episode of *Ulysses*, perhaps the main intertext to the play. Moreover, Johnston's drama is similar to O'Casey's in its

[18] Christine St. Peter also identifies the other two artists caricatured ("O'Rooney" and "O'Mooney") as prose writer Liam O'Flaherty and painter Patrick Tuohy respectively. Johnston, *The Old Lady*, 93, 104.

[19] The satirical treatment of O'Casey has been noted by almost all the writers on the play.

deconstruction of heroism, an effect which is, however, achieved by rather different means. The mockery of heroism is of course apparent from the very beginning of the ridiculous, over-pompous and over-sentimental melodrama with which *The Old Lady* opens. The melodrama pretends to dramatise the final days in the life of Robert Emmet, yet the lines attributed to him are a combination of borrowings from dated political poetry, Emmet's actual speech from the dock, and even plays by Yeats, Lady Gregory and Shaw.[20] This textual compound is later also enriched by fragments of Pearse's funeral oration at the grave of O'Donovan Rossa and a few lines attributed to Charles Stuart Parnell. This makes the Speaker (i.e., the Emmet character in the play) appear to be on the one hand a "generic patriot"[21] of the Republican variety; on the other, his manifestly textual nature would surely make him an ideal character for any self-respecting postmodern writer.

The self-assured identity of the hero dissolves shortly after he has received the inadvertent blow from the butt of a gun, as he is revealed to be a mere actor. For the rest of the play, his identity fluctuates freely between that of Robert Emmet and that of an actor, while the preceding meta-dramatic moment foregrounds the fact that this fuzzy character himself is only an actor in a play they are watching. The two levels of the (meta)drama intermingle freely, both through individual characters and particular lines from the initial melodrama, making the setting, plot and characters of the play difficult to pin down. The problematic nature of the hero's identity is continually emphasised throughout the play, as the issue emerges again and again, and especially in moments of critical importance to him:

OLDER MAN: This chap says he's Robert Emmet.
SPEAKER: I am.
OLDER MAN: Oh, you are, are you?

---

[20] Cf. Johnston, *The Old Lady*, 57-62.
[21] Canfield, "A Note on the Nature of Expressionism," 39.

SPEAKER: I am.

OLDER MAN: Well answer me this then. *What's happened to your boots?*

This is the point at which the Speaker discovers he is suddenly wearing carpet slippers instead; he is completely at a loss:

SPEAKER: I don't know ... I thought they were ... I see your point ... I ...

VOICES: Well?

SPEAKER: Perhaps I had better explain ... You see ... someone took them from me when I was playing Robert Emmet and ...

OLDER MAN (*with heavy sarcasm*) Oh so you were *playing* Robert Emmet? A play-actor are you? [48]

Throughout the remaining part of the play, the slippered Speaker in fact wanders through caricatured contemporary Dublin as a "Don Quixote Alighieri" (57), fumbling with his identity and heroic vocation in the same way as he is physically fumbling with the folds of a curtain (38). He constantly searches for a "plain ... clear and simple" free Ireland (45) as envisaged in his time, and simultaneously for his idealised lover Sarah Curran. The critique of heroism that the play offers also has its other side then, represented by the quixotic quality of the Speaker's quest, which betrays a measure of sympathy for the man of action, be he a misguided, tragicomic figure.

The feeling of pity for the bootless "hero" is strengthened by the image of Dublin that the play puts forward. The very first encounter with a passer-by demonstrates to the Speaker the un-idealistic, business-like nature of the present:

SPEAKER: (*now in the midst of the traffic*): Men of Eire, awake to be blest! Do you hear? (*He fiercely accosts a PASSER-BY.*) Do you hear? Awake!

PASSER-BY (*politely disengaging himself*): Sorry. The banks close at half two. [33]

The Speaker's Messianic urge simply fails to resonate any longer. The ideals that people like him had been fighting for have now been entirely commodified, which becomes most poignantly apparent when some of the side characters start organising bus trips to the utopian realms of the Heart's Desire:

> TWO TOUTS (*distributing handbills*): Next bus leaves in ten minutes. All aboard for Tir-na-n'Og. Special reduced return fares at single and a third. The Radio Train for Hy Brasail. No waits. No stops. Courtesy, efficiency and punctuality. Joneses Road, Walsh Road, Philipsburgh Avenue, Clontarf, Clonturk, Curran's Cross and the New Jerusalem. [46]

The commodification of ideals is shown to go hand-in-hand with pretence and corruption, as is apparent in Part Two, which opens with a high-society party where a number of pretentious, hypocritical characters are listening to a Minister's daughter lisping "Kingth Bweakfatht," an English children's poem by A.A. Milne learnt at The Banba School of Acting, Lower Abbey Street (53-54). The guests there include three state-supported artists, O'Cooney, O'Mooney and O'Rooney,[22] complemented by the statue of the constitutional nationalist politician Henry Grattan, as the Minister and his wife always take great care to "have a few of the nicest statues in on Sunday evening" (59). The statue, however, speaks with the voice of the notorious Major Sirr, the officer responsible for the arrest of Robert Emmet. The Minister for Arts and Crafts himself actually "bears a strange resemblance" to the dim-witted Stage Hand of the first part (54), while the celebrated Free State General has emerged from the Redcoat who knocked out Robert Emmet in the introductory melodrama. But, as a stage remark claims, the atmosphere is "all very nice indeed" (54). Johnston deliberately employs the same actors to play different characters, largely to stress the corrupt nature of the social elite, and also merely to provide some merriment.

---

[22] See above, 90 and note 18.

All in all, *The Old Lady*'s mockery is directed not only at the pathetic heroism of people like Robert Emmet, whose rising for the freedom of Ireland was a spectacular fiasco and managed only to put a final seal on the Union with Britain for over a hundred years. It is also the present state of affairs which is deeply criticised. On the other hand, the sympathy apparent in the treatment of those who rise to act is equalled by the final alleviation of negative feeling towards contemporary Dublin: after the climactic scene in the brothel-like tenement, the sham city receives an unexpected pardon from the Speaker:

> Strumpet city in the sunset
> Suckling the bastard brats of Scots, of Englishry, of Huguenot.
> Brave sons breaking from the womb, wild sons fleeing from their Mother.
> Wilful city of savage dreamers,
> So old, so sick with memories!
> Old Mother
> Some they say are damned,
> But you, I know, will walk the streets of Paradise
> Head high, and unashamed. [78]

Although it is certainly possible to view this slightly decadent tribute—described by Harold Ferrar as "an impassionate offering to Dublin by a bruised lover"[23]—in an ironic light, particularly in view of the Speaker's earlier proclamations that appeared to be totally irrelevant, self-centred and/or sentimental, the emotional power of the scene virtually prevents one from perceiving them as ironic. Curtis Canfield was certainly justified in claiming that "the author's pen [...] stabs vindictively into both" the romantic idealism and the "wretched present";[24] however, in both cases there is just that minute residuum of understanding for both.

---

23 Ferrar, *Denis Johnston's Irish Theatre*, 19.
24 Canfield, "A Note on the Nature of Expressionism," 45. Or, in Nicholas Grene's words, the play is "poised somewhere between satiric debunking of the claims

One of the most subversive aspects of the play lies undoubtedly in its treatment of the allegorical female embodiment of Ireland. First of all, the identity of the woman is again subverted by the fact that the character moves freely between Cathleen ni Houlihan or the Shan Van Vocht, Emmet's idealised lover Sarah Curran, the legendary Deirdre and a bawdy Flower Woman (the appellative Sarah ni Hooligan coined by the author later in his life seems indeed a most appropriate summary),[25] all played by the same actress. The "Old Lady" appears in the play first as a tattered vendor of violets, whose introductory utterance itself refers to the allegorical motive, while being at the same time a biting satire of Yeats's and Lady Gregory's *Cathleen ni Houlihan*: "Me four bewtyful gre-in fields. Me four bewtyful gre-in fields" (36). Presently, the woman starts offering her four green fields for sale together with her merchandise, and finally resorts to plain begging: "God bless ye, lovely gentlemen, spare a copper for a cuppa tea" (37).

The Speaker's reaction is one of horror, as he eventually recognises Sarah Curran in this terrible apparition (it is the same voice, albeit with a different accent and diction). The identification is made explicit in Part Two; however, shortly after the first encounter with the Speaker, the woman begins to behave in a lascivious manner, demanding her "rights," while the ultimate one is the Speaker's blood, "the cheapest thing the good God has made" (47). When her vampiric wish is not granted,[26] she points out in a rage that he is not the heroic Emmet at all but a mere actor.

The forceful disruption of the nationalist allegory takes on another turn in the tenement scene mentioned, in which the woman brazenly behaves like a bawd most of the time, while

of the revolution and satiric exposure of the society that has failed to live up to those claims." Grene, *The Politics of Irish Drama*, 154.

25 Johnston, *Orders and Desecrations*, 69.

26 This may indeed constitute the very first version of Cathleen ni Houlihan as a vampire. Cf. also the first chapter of the present work, page 33.

also fiercely rejecting Joe's death, and the death of her two other "sons" present, for her:

> JOE: (*through his teeth*): Strumpet! Strumpet!
> WOMAN: Blast ye! ye'd use that word t'yer own mudher, would ye! God, I'll throttle ye with me own two hands for the dirty scut ye are!
> [...]
> JOE (*very soft*): Well ... so long, lads. It was ... a grand life ... so long, lad ... that plugged me ... So long ... (*He dies.*)
> WOMAN: Burn ye! Burn ye! [...] One son with th' divil in hell, an' two more with th' divils on earth. (*She spits.*) God forgive me for weanin' a brood a sorry scuts! [71-73]

However, after she has received from the Government a token kitschy gift of flowers embedded in plastic, she seems to be happy and responds to the glorification of Joe with melodramatic keening:

> Sure, it's them we love th' best is took th' first, God help us.
> Ullagone! Ullagone! Ochone-a-ree! [...]
> Low lie your heads this day
> My sons! My sons!
> The strong in their pride go by me
> Saying, "Where are thy sons?"
> [...]
> Gall to our heart! Oh, gall to our heart!
> Ullagone! Ochone-a-ree!
> A lost dream to us now in our home! [74-75]

The meaning of this passage is again double-edged. The parody of the keening Woman of Ireland is apparent, as is the satire that springs from her false motives; nonetheless, the woman is in fact also right in pointing out that courage, patriotism and idealistic dreaming are gone from contemporary Ireland. She in fact cuts a tragic figure at the same time, as noted already by Grattan in Part One:

All of us fit to lead, and none of us fit to serve. [...] Driven blindly on by the fury of our spurious moral courage! Is there to be no rest for Ireland from her soul? What monstrous blasphemy has she committed to be condemned to drift for ever like the wandering Jew after a Heaven that can never be? [38]

It seems that the present people of Ireland are to blame for not letting the allegorical woman lie down to rest for ever. But again, even these words cannot be taken as an absolute statement, since they are in fact uttered by a statue, and moreover the statue of an opponent of the central character for whom the audience cannot help but feel a degree of pity. Furthermore, the woman is revealed in the course of the play as a character who is indeed far from the dignified image of the wandering Jew.

The satirical treatment of the Woman of Ireland in *The Old Lady* cuts in all directions: against militant nationalists and utopian dreamers, against the revival of the image in plays such as *Cathleen ni Houlihan* ("Hoopsie-daisie! The walk of a Quee-in!" chants the tattered hag [47]), but there is also a shade of indictment aimed at the materialism of contemporary Ireland which let Cathleen degenerate into a lewd old beggar. Throughout all this, however, the character still remains allegorical, standing for an Ireland that says "No!" both to nationalist heroes and to the current political and cultural leaders.

Although it may appear that language is predominantly shaped by expressionist techniques in this context, it still performs a crucial role. Not only is much of the play's meaning based on intertextual references (which makes *The Old Lady* delightful to read for the inquisitive scholar but rather more demanding to watch, particularly for a non-contemporaneous and/or non-Irish audience): one of the aims of the play is to explode the rhetoric of militant romantic nationalism, together with the kind of Irish literary drama written by the likes of Yeats, Synge and O'Casey. This is done consistently throughout the play, while one of the fundamental means of deflation is the creation of a brilliant, ironical linguistic collage.

Moreover, the play thematises an inquiry into the relationship between certain words and deeds. In a political argument during a game of cards, the Younger Man claims that Irish political emancipation was achieved because the likes of him had the courage to shout "Up the Republic!" again and again. To this the Older Man angrily retorts "Aw, that's all words. Nothing but bloody words. You can't change the world by words." But the former responds by developing his argument further:

> That's where you fool yourself! What other way can you change it? I tell you, we can make this country—this world—whatever we want it to be by saying so, and saying so again. I tell you it is the knowledge of this that is the genius and glory of the Gael! [70]

A bold statement indeed. It seems that the author in his "A Note on What Happened" acknowledged to a certain degree the argument of the Younger Man, suggesting that with "the Emmets in particular" and "intransigent Irish Republicanism in general [...] 'The Republic still lives' is not an expression of a pious hope, but is in itself a creative act, as England knows to her cost."[27] Nevertheless, the play undermines the Younger Man's claim in several ways: the context of gambling in which it is uttered is difficult to ignore, as is the pathetic, alliterative wording of the final line. The play also shows that the state which resulted from the struggle of the supporters of freedom is indeed far from the intended Republic of Paradise.

The rhetoric of the Speaker/Emmet (in whose tradition the Diehard Younger Man follows) is indeed shown to be ridiculous to a much larger degree; however, the character is one of the few in the play who are ready to act on their words. Profoundly perturbed by the world that surrounds him, the

[27] Johnston, "A Note on What Happened," 84.

Speaker mounts a final effort in which he exorcises the Shadows of the country's wise and attempts to conjure up the utopian realm of his mind, together with his beloved Sarah Curran:

> Cursed be he who values the life above the dream. [...] Cursed be he who builds but does not destroy. [...] Cursed be he who honours the wisdom of the wise. [...] Cursed be the ear that heeds the prayer of the dead. [...] Cursed be the eye that sees the heart of a foe. [...] Cursed be prayers that plough not, praises that reap not, joys that laugh not, sorrows that weep not. [...] I will take this earth in both my hands and batter it into the semblance of my heart's desire! See, there by the trees is reared the gable of the house where sleeps my dear one. Under my feet the grass is growing, soft and subtle, in the evening dew. The cool, clean wind is blowing down from Killakee, kissing my hair and dancing with the flowers that fill the garden all around me. And Sarah ... Sarah Curran ... you are there ... waiting for Robert Emmet.
>
> I know this garden well for I have called it into being with the Credo of the Invincibles: I believe in the might of Creation, the majesty of the Will, the resurrection of the Word, and Birth Everlasting. [77-78]

The speech combines the language of Anglican liturgy with that of Blake's "Proverbs of Hell," but also aligns itself with the Credo of the Invincibles, a secret terrorist group responsible for the Phoenix Park assassination of the British Chief Secretary Lord Cavendish and his undersecretary in 1882.[28] Here, the Speaker displays patent nationalist militancy and blindness. At the same time, what he in fact does is require of words to act. His desire is to turn certain words into a peculiar kind of performatives, and ultimately have language bring about a

---

[28] D.E.S. Maxwell has pointed out that the final passages of *The Old Lady* draw upon "Emmet's speech from the dock, the resurrection thesis of the Litany, and the Commination service of the Anglican church." Maxwell, *A Critical History of Modern Irish Drama*, 117. The allusion to Blake is specified by Christine St. Peter. Cf. Johnston, *The Old Lady*, 121-22.

pastoral. But powerful as his invocation is, its collapse is all the greater.

Vigorously opposing Blake's aphoristic exclamations,[29] the Speaker's call is for prayers to plough, praises to reap, joys to laugh and sorrows to weep. This hopeless cry only sums up the nature of the Speaker's enterprise,[30] and also qualifies the act of verbal sorcery that follows it, as the rhetorical and emotional force of that act could otherwise be easily succumbed to. And there are further aspects which disrupt the conjuring gesture. The fervent urge to battle is supplemented by the violence entailed in the creation of the pastoral ("I will take this earth in both my hands and batter it into the semblance of my heart's desire!"),[31] while it is ultimately the very ending of the play that discards the sham conjuror together with his powerful vision, as the Speaker slowly dissolves into the actor from the first part which he really is (while that actor is presently going to turn into a real actor himself, asking for applause). Should one need a further irony, the contrary effect of the historical Robert Emmet's vision and rhetoric can be recalled once more: the only "achievement" of Emmet's rising was the killing of the remarkably impartial judge Lord Justice Kilwarden by a mob.

To put it simply, idealist, heroic rhetoric is paraded in all its emotional power, yet it is disclosed as necessarily entailing

---

[29] "Prayers plow not! Praises reap not!/ Joys laugh not! Sorrows weep not!" William Blake, *The Marriage of Heaven and Hell*, Plate 9, *Selected Poetry*, ed. W.H. Stevenson (Harmondsworth: Penguin, 1988) 70.

[30] What the play *performs* about language has been since described at length by philosophers: the most detailed treatment of performatives as opposed to statements is that of J.L. Austin in his *How to Do Things with Words* (New York: Oxford University Press, 1962). The minute analysis of particular words and situations in which these can perform particular actions has, however, frequently brought Austin into a blind alley, while Jacques Derrida has poignantly shown that Austin's difficulties arise precisely because the notion of the performative is bound with the notions of intention and fully determined context. Jacques Derrida, "Signature Event Context," *Margins of Philosophy*, trans. Alan Bass (Brighton: Harvester, 1982).

[31] The line paraphrases stanza 73 of the *Rubaiyat of Omar Khayyam*, replacing the "moulding" of the world according to the Heart's desire with a much more violent image. Cf. Johnston, *The Old Lady*, 122, 20.

violence and hatred, while its effect is shown to be far from the original intention (if indeed there is any effect at all). Words of particular nationalists and their heroes may in themselves be a "creative act" but what gets eventually created is hardly a pastoral. Despite this, *The Old Lady* does not strive to propound a political alternative: in Harold Ferrar's words, "Johnston offers no way out of the political mess made by yesterday's heroes. The satirical purpose of the play is to provide the beginning of an awareness that there is a mess" and in order to clean it up: "The first step [...] must be excision of the dead tissue of romance and melodrama in national life."[32]

The complex of subversive ironic impulses makes Johnston's *The Old Lady* the play to have demonstrated most poignantly — even more so than Sean O'Casey's *The Silver Tassie* — that the initial era of the Irish national theatre at the Abbey was over. *The Old Lady* not only radically criticises nationalist heroism, but also abandons the tradition of the Abbey Irish play for extensive experimentalism, questioning the idea of the Abbey narrative drama as an adequate means of representing national identity on the stage. Through its use of expressionist techniques and the method of collage it does not, however, necessarily aim to put itself forward as *the* alternative. What it does is merely to stress, generally in an amusing manner, the necessity of a search for different dramatic methods, and ultimately perhaps also different themes.

Overviewing the long list of subversive moments in Johnston's "satire of national immaturity,"[33] it is small wonder that the Abbey would not have *The Old Lady* on its stage. And despite the fact that Yeats's diplomatic approach managed to bring Johnston into the National Theatre with his next play, *The Moon in the Yellow River*, the rejection of *The Old Lady* confirmed very clearly that if there were plays that approached political topics in an innovative manner, they were no longer to be seen at the Abbey. The plan to make the Irish national theatre the site

---

[32] Ferrar, *Denis Johnston's Irish Theatre*, 39.
[33] Ferrar, *Denis Johnston's Irish Theatre*, 19.

of free experimentation, expressed in the original statement of its objectives by the Irish Literary Theatre, had been as good as abandoned,[34] and the professed desire to encourage innovative Irish plays may be viewed only in an ironic light by this phase of the National Theatre's history. It is true that Yeats eventually came to change his views about expressionism in drama, the Abbey did finally stage O'Casey's *The Silver Tassie* in 1935, thus creating a public row and an internal controversy among NTS members,[35] but there was really no substantial change of general direction. The Abbey Theatre was to remain a realm of conservative dramaturgy and stereotypical theatre practice until the arrival of the new generation of talented playwrights in the 1960s.

---

[34] Cf. also Grene, *The Politics of Irish Drama*, 138.

[35] Yeats's decision to give the green light to the play testifies to the influence of new modernist drama and his reappraisal of Toller's work. Foster, *W.B. Yeats: A Life*, II.525. The Abbey production of *The Silver Tassie* initiated loud protests by Catholic groups and the Gaelic League who claimed the play was blasphemous and obscene (significantly, *not* that it challenged their politics), while Catholic writer Brinsley MacNamara resigned from the Abbey board. For more details, see Foster, *W.B. Yeats: A Life*, II.525, 532; Dean, *Riot and Great Anger*, 132; Pilkington, *Theatre and the State*, 126-31.

III. REVISIONS

history and the current situation. In Lyotard's view, these metanarratives are ultimately dangerous, since they have been responsible for most atrocities committed in the twentieth century. Hence, they should be abandoned, and the world should ideally turn into a place inhabited solely by particular micro-narratives. Such individual stories should be involved not in the dialectic of a dialogue—as the search for truth in a world of discourse has been one of the main reasons for the emergence of perilous metanarratives—but in a large number of language games whose rules would be subject to constant change by these individual stories.[2]

Although Lyotard's line of argument may be intriguing, it does not specify how to move from the current situation to a world composed of individual narratives. Lyotard is basically not concerned with established patterns of interaction between existing narratives, large or small. The history of Field Day may be seen to convey, once again, a crucial message regarding the central evasion in Lyotard's vision, particularly since Brian Friel's work as its leading author has maintained a steady and detailed focus on patterns of human interaction.

In order to address its general concerns with discursivity, communication, and ultimately also the relevance of post-colonial approaches to Ireland, the present analysis aims to provide a survey of the dramatic work of Brian Friel from the appropriate period, and to assess the general ideas of Field Day as formulated by Seamus Deane and Friel bearing in mind the insights evident in Friel's plays. I will commence by examining Field Day's approach to the issue of representing Ireland, looking particularly at the (re)emergence of metanarratives in texts dealing with national identity. This will lead into a detailed discussion of Brian Friel's approach to interpersonal communication as an inherent aspect of any discursive context. Friel's treatment of communication inadequacies and failures will then be referred back to the general theoretical issues

---

[2] Jean-François Lyotard, *La condition postmoderne* (Paris: Editions de Minuit, 1979) Ch. 14 passim.

outlined above, and serve as a commentary on their relevance to 1980s Ireland facing an impasse in Northern Ireland.

(Re)Shaping Ireland

Judging by Brian Friel's "history plays" staged by Field Day, Friel may appear to be a playwright whose main concern is not historical accuracy. It has been noted, for instance, that the historical events in the early play *The Freedom of the City* (1974) have been shifted by two years. Moreover, at least two historians, including the author of one of Friel's sources, have pointed out—together with the majority of Field Day's opponents—various factual inaccuracies in *Translations* (1980), mainly discussing how the Donegal hedge school and the Ordnance Survey were represented.[3] Finally, in *Making History* (1988), Friel not only significantly condensed the events of ten years into slightly under two, but in the programme notes to the play he introduces something that Sean Connolly has called "a subtle practical joke at the expense of the hapless academic fact checker":[4] the playwright makes an elaborate apology for allowing Mabel Bagenal to live for ten years longer, while giving a false date for her actual death and miscalculating the passing of time within the play.

Plays are certainly not supposed to be viewed as history books. As Friel himself has said, "Drama is first a fiction, with the authority of fiction. You don't go to Macbeth for history."[5] Nevertheless, the situation of Friel's Field Day plays with a

3 See "Translations and A Paper Landscape: Between Fiction and History: Brian Friel, John Andrews and Kevin Barry," *Crane Bag* 7.2 (1983): 118-24; J.H. Andrews, "Notes for a Future Edition of Brian Friel's Translations," *Irish Review* 13 (1992-93): 93-106; Sean Connolly, "Translating History: Brian Friel and the Irish Past," *The Achievement of Brian Friel*, ed. Alan Peacock (Gerrards Cross: Colin Smythe, 1993) 151-53.
4 Connolly, "Translating History," 159-60.
5 "Translations and A Paper Landscape," quoted in *Brian Friel. Essays, Diaries, Interviews: 1964-1999*, ed. Christopher Murray (London and New York: Faber, 1999) 119.

historical setting is peculiar in that they were presented as part of an effort to revise entrenched versions of Irish history, while their relevance to 1980s Ireland is fairly self-evident. Combined with the fact that plays such as *Translations* or *Making History* overtly specify their precise setting in time, one can see why the historians were provoked into criticising Friel for twisting history. Moreover, Ulf Dantanus suggested in the mid-1980s that some critics' impatience of with Friel simply proved that there was still an overwhelming demand for realist drama about Ireland, i.e., drama that would treat history in an objectivist way.[6]

What needs to be apprehended above all is the myth-making potential of some aspects of the plays. The attempt to redefine the Irish past in itself implies that myths and stereotypes inherent in existing versions of the country's history be dispelled. This is explicitly acknowledged in one of the early Field Day pamphlets, Richard Kearney's "Myth and Motherland,"[7] while it can be inferred also from Seamus Deane's early texts. Nonetheless, even Roland Barthes, the originator of the current notion of demythologisation, was well aware of the fact that dispelling myths always entails creating new ones.[8] The analysis of Friel's representation of Irish history attempted below will help to outline the nature of these new myths.

Before addressing the issue of myth in Friel's Field Day plays, however, careful consideration should be given to their context within the project. A similar analysis will also be required in the case of the Field Day justifications by Seamus Deane *vis-à-vis* the results of Field Day's effort. Field Day begins

6 Ulf Dantanus, *Brian Friel: The Growth of an Irish Dramatist* (Acta Universitatis Gothoburgensis: Göteborg, 1985) 183.
7 Richard Kearney, "Myth and Motherland," Field Day Theatre Company, *Ireland's Field Day* (London: Hutchinson, 1985) 59-80.
8 Roland Barthes, *Mythologies*, trans. Annette Lavers (New York: Hill and Wang, 1972) 156-59; cf. also Roland Barthes, "Mythology Today," *The Rustle of Language*, trans. Richard Howard (Berkeley and Los Angeles: University of California Press, 1989) 65-68.

to define itself in a more detailed way in the first series of pamphlets authored by a number of critics and artists which are loosely connected by more or less implicit common objectives.[9] This documents an overall tendency not to create a new metanarrative but rather to give voice to a plurality of individual micro-narratives. For a movement that aims at a critique of current stereotypes pertinent to the Irish situation, such a predisposition seems most appropriate. In "Heroic Styles: The Tradition of an Idea," Seamus Deane claims that "A literature predicated on an abstract idea of essence—Irishness or Ulsterness—will inevitably degenerate into whimsy and provincialism," while any such idea, i.e., foundation of a metanarrative, may potentially represent significant danger, especially if applied in the North. The inherited tradition has to be revised, he continues, while the Irish have to stop being so quick "to accept the mystique of Irishness as an inalienable feature of [their] writing and, indeed, of much else in [their] culture."[10]

However, Deane also asserts in the same pamphlet that "it is impossible to do without ideas of a tradition. But it is necessary to disengage from the traditions of the ideas which the literary revival and the accompanying political revolution sponsored so successfully."[11] This clearly suggests that only a particular kind of tradition is to be rejected, while the notion of tradition itself must be retained. A question naturally arises: does this in itself not entail the formation of a metanarrative? And, what is to be the specific idea that should serve as the basis for the (re)formation of the Irish tradition?

Deane's answer in "Heroic Styles" is that first, "Everything, including [Irish] politics and [Irish] literature, has to be rewritten, i.e., re-read. [This] will enable new writing, new politics, unblemished by Irishness, but securely Irish."[12] Deane

9 Published jointly as *Ireland's Field Day* in 1985.
10 Seamus Deane, "Heroic Styles: The Tradition of an Idea," *Ireland's Field Day*, 57.
11 Deane, "Heroic Styles," 56.
12 Deane, "Heroic Styles," 58.

does not make any such formative idea explicit; the preceding brief analysis and the paradoxical "securely Irish" ending of the pamphlet seem to suggest that a re-examination of the material will automatically give rise to an underlying idea of this kind. The notion of plurality of discourses is also disqualified by Deane's insistence on the use of the first person plural throughout his pamphlet. Clearly, there is a desire for unity, albeit perhaps not necessarily for dominance. Despite this, the tendency of Field Day to return to common Irish origins, combined with its stress on the need for "decolonisation" may be seen to align it with Republicanism/nationalism.[13]

Deane's "General Introduction" to the *Field Day Anthology of Irish Writing* makes much more clearly manifest the tension that is already apparent in the early pamphlets.[14] Deane begins by stressing that the anthology represents "no attempt [...] to establish a canon," while he also emphasises "the fictive nature of any tradition that asserts continuity while acknowledging its need to do so." Nevertheless, he insists that "there *is* a story here, a metanarrative" which Field Day believe to be "hospitable to all the micro-narratives that, from time to time, have achieved prominence as the official version of the true history, political and literary, of the island's past and present."[15] While it certainly has to be acknowledged that the space provided by *any* anthology is necessarily limited, thus making it inevitable to select certain individual micro-narratives to be represented,[16] the criterion of "prominence" seems to be quite

13 Cf. Edna Longley, *From Cathleen to Anorexia* (Dublin: The Attic Press, 1990) 12, 13.

14 As a matter of fact, contradictions quite similar to those of Deane's "Heroic Styles" also appear in Richard Kearney's "Myth and Motherland": witness, for instance, the call for a re-mythologisation of the past where the new myths must be constantly in dialogue with history while "objective" history is at the same time implicitly shown to be an impossibility.

15 Seamus Deane, "General Introduction," *The Field Day Anthology of Irish Writing*, ed. Seamus Deane (Derry: Field Day, 1991) xix. Further references appear in parentheses in the text.

16 Which is an issue that Deane duly addresses. Cf. Deane, "General Introduction," xx.

striking if the proclaimed aim is a fundamental revision of the past, while the notorious lack of women's voices in Volumes I-III of the anthology requires no further comment in this context.[17] The claim to the existence of an underlying metanarrative deserves special attention, particularly when read in conjunction with the rejection of metanarratives that stress a need for continuity. Assuming that any narrative, including the one behind the anthology, has to maintain a certain degree of continuity in order to be called thus, the following question seems quite legitimate: does this mean the only difference between, say, the initially denounced metanarrative of the Literary Revival and the one of Field Day rests in the sole fact that the latter does not make the need for continuity explicit? There is undoubtedly an important strategic reason for a clear distinction between the two projects. Nevertheless, it is apparent that a theoretical justification of this kind may ironically turn precisely against the intended strategy.

The final paragraph of the Introduction specifies the idea of the Field Day metanarrative as follows:

> If we could claim that in every corner of the anthology one could find contained, *in parvo*, the whole scheme and meaning of it, then our ambitions would be fulfilled. But if the scheme of the anthology is not so discovered, we have little doubt that some alternative to it will be revealed, whatever page is opened, whatever work or excerpt is read. It is the endless fecundity of such reading that gives justification to the selections with which we here attempt to define our subject. [xxvi]

---

[17] Despite this, the present author would not like to join the line of the critics who have focused, as Richard Kirkland has observed, more on the editors and on the Field Day enterprise than on the content of the three volumes itself. Richard Kirkland, *Literature and Culture in Northern Ireland since 1965: Moments of Danger* (London and New York: Addison Wesley Longman, 1996) 141. The anthology certainly provides a thorough introduction to Irish literature and culture and is the best available up to date, especially after the publication of the additional Volumes IV and V focused on women's writing (2002).

The invitation of a plurality of all the metanarratives that the readers might find is definitely laudable. Despite this, it seems questionable simply to assume that the readers' metanarratives resulting from their interpretation of the material will automatically be in accord with the Field Day metanarrative itself; this problem was at least partially revealed in many reviews of the anthology. The presumable openness is disqualified by three crucial features of the anthology and its Introduction: by the fact of selection/marginalisation, the admission to a particular Field Day metanarrative and, once again, a rhetoric which seems to imply totalisation—the use of expressions such as "our own history," or describing Irish literature as "autonomous, ordered" (xxvi).

Unlike most authors of the Field Day pamphlets, Brian Friel has always been interested predominantly in individual people and their emotions, in their micro-narratives and their position within the surrounding discourse. Nevertheless, with Field Day he embarked on a project which explicitly focused on re-examining current myths and metanarratives; this certainly had an impact on his approach. His involvement in Field Day was also the main reason why he gave several of his otherwise rare interviews around the time of the first Field Day production— *Translations*. In one of these, he notably spoke about Field Day as "an artistic fifth province" (using an idea originally suggested by Richard Kearney)[18] rising above and covering the whole island of Ireland, while not accepting any simplified and entrenched North-South division. He saw the objective of Field Day in terms of looking for "some kind of sense of the country, what is this island about, north and south, and what are our attitudes to it."[19] A month or so later he remarked that the Field Day project "should lead to a cultural state, not a political state.

[18] Patrick Quilligan, "Field Day's New Double Bill," *The Irish Times* 18 Sept. 1984, reprinted in *Brian Friel in Conversation*, ed. Paul Delaney (Ann Arbor: The University of Michigan Press, 2000) 193.

[19] Ray Comiskey, "Rehearsing Friel's New Farce," *The Irish Times* 14 Sept. 1982, reprinted in *Brian Friel in Conversation*, 165.

And [...] out of that cultural state, a possibility of a political state follows."[20]

The notions of an all-encompassing fifth province and the cultural state imply an underlying metanarrative, one which asserts that art can function as a unifying political force. As is the case with Seamus Deane, the metanarrative is never made explicit by Friel, be it in his work or in his own statements about it. What *is* explicit, on the other hand, is the action that this metanarrative seems to prompt: a search for and an analysis of the meta- or micro-narratives currently present in Ireland, a country whose state Friel terms "confusion."[21]

Friel's treatment of history in his Field Day plays may frequently give rise to particular myths concerning the Irish past, as noted earlier. These myths, while not necessarily epitomising a consistent metanarrative as yet, could potentially provide the basis for one. Friel seems to be quite aware of this danger, as he often attempts to carefully balance what could be viewed as mythologisations with suitable qualifications. A case in point is how Friel handles the Irish hedge school in *Translations*. To an extent, the criticism of the politics here appears to be just. Not because of the fact that such a school could not have existed: research in this area shows that there really may have been hedge schools which taught not only basic reading and writing skills but also Latin and Greek, although such schools would clearly have been an exception.[22] What is significant, however, is that even if the play ceases to be

20 Fintan O'Toole, "The Man from God Knows Where: Interview with Brian Friel," *In Dublin* 165 (28 Oct. 1982), reprinted in *Brian Friel in Conversation*, 175.
21 Paddy Agnew, "'Talking to Ourselves,'" *Magill* Dec. 1980: 61. It is interesting to note how Friel's use of the term here almost ironically echoes its remarkable occurrence in a positive context in *Translations*: Hugh claims in a much-quoted speech that "confusion is not an ignoble condition." Brian Friel, *Selected Plays* (London and Boston: Faber, 1984) 446. Further references appear in parentheses in the text.
22 Sean Connolly, who is critical of Friel's depiction of the hedge schools, quotes the relevant statistics in detail. However, even these do not completely disprove the existence of a school similar to Hugh O'Donnell's. "Translating History," 152.

regarded as a mirror image of reality, the hedge school will still stand out as a distinct allegory of a culture in decline, an allegory that exhibits a considerable degree of nostalgia for an ancient learned civilisation which has to give way to a materialist world of commerce and warfare.

The representation of the Ordnance Survey in *Translations* is somewhat similar in its bias to Friel's treatment of the hedge school. Friel has been criticised for turning an operation whose intentions were predominantly economic and whose form was in general peaceful into an act of imperial power. In this instance, the playwright did indeed commit what are plainly errors of fact, such as equipping the sappers with bayonets or having their captain order livestock to be killed, houses to be burnt down and other people's tenants to be evicted.[23] Commenting on this issue, Friel remarked sardonically: "I feel very lucky that I have been corrected only for using a few misplaced bayonets and for suggesting that British soldiers might have been employed to evict peasants."[24] His dismissal might make sense as a defence of liberties being taken for the sake of dramatic plausibility; however, as a result, the English soldiers in the play come to represent a violent (and unlearned)[25] force which delivers a decisive blow to an ancient Gaelic civilisation. Although it is difficult to read their military revenge *only* as an invasion of ruthless armed barbarians into an age-old realm of poetic culture since the indigenous culture is presented as being already in an advanced state of decay and the British Army thus only administer to it a final blow,[26] it cannot be denied that *Translations* reiterates particular myths/stereotypes about the role of the insensitive English in

---

[23] Connolly, "Translating History," 152-53, 157.

[24] "*Translations* and *A Paper Landscape*," quoted in Murray, *Brian Friel. Essays, Diaries, Interviews*, 116.

[25] A reviewer for the London *Sunday Times*, for instance, expressed righteous indignation at the English officer Lancey being unable to recognise even a few basic words of Latin. *Sunday Times*, 28 Sept. 1980, quoted in Pilkington, *Theatre and the State*, 212.

[26] Connolly, "Translating History," 155.

the passing of a superior Gaelic culture. This impression is only supported by Captain Lancey's violent attack on the symbolic figure of Sarah, "shawled" in the manner of Yeats and Lady Gregory's Cathleen ni Houlihan, who consequently loses her newly acquired ability to speak.[27]

There are several more features of *Translations* which may be interpreted as mythologisations, although with these the situation is more complex and counter-arguments may easily be raised. One of these features is the manner in which the language of the Irish is handled:

> HUGH: Indeed, Lieutenant. A rich language. A rich literature. You'll find, sir, that certain cultures expend on their vocabularies and syntax acquisitive energies and ostentations entirely lacking in their material lives. I suppose you could call us a spiritual people. [...] Yes, it is a rich language, Lieutenant, full of the mythologies of fantasy and hope and self-deception—a syntax opulent with tomorrows. It is our response to mud cabins and a diet of potatoes; our only method of replying to ... inevitabilities. [418-19]

So far the much-quoted passage from Hugh's speech to Yolland. Ulf Dantanus has correctly pointed out that although it may seem to be a commentary, albeit rather a sarcastic one, on how flowery the Irish language is, Hugh is actually speaking rather voluble English at this moment.[28] This irony tends to dissolve the suspicion that the play promotes the Revivalist myth of the superiority of Irish to English.

Nevertheless, the alleged influence of material squalor on the richness of speech has so far been read almost as a statement from a scientific treatise of authority, and its validity has been taken for granted. This may perhaps be due to the fact that it is backed up by the views of George Steiner (the core of the first paragraph above being almost a literal quote from his

---

27 Pilkington, *Theatre and the State*, 212.
28 Dantanus, *Brian Friel*, 178.

After Babel, as noted by several commentators).[29] The whole idea, and particularly its relevance to the Irish context, still remains to be analysed though, while there have certainly been some prominent opposing voices—suffice it to mention, for instance, Myles na gCopaleen's satirical treatment of such a view in *The Poor Mouth*.[30]

In fact, Steiner's view does not feature in the play as a simple statement of truth. This becomes apparent when we examine the dramatic situation in which the above-mentioned speech is uttered. Hugh is by no means reading from a book of authority. Instead, he is described in a stage direction as "almost self-consciously jaunty and alert. Indeed, as the scene progresses, one has the sense that he is deliberately parodying himself" (416-17). At the same time, he is trying to show off in front of Yolland. There are several reasons behind his behaviour: undoubtedly the return of his anglicised son, the English presence in the village itself, his nursing of a severe hangover from the previous night and, last but not least, the fact that he is about to purposely abandon his thirty years of teaching through Irish and accept a position in an English-language National school.[31] Such a context indeed lends a touch of ambiguity to his elevated statements, thus disabling the passage from being read as a mere reiteration of a nationalist myth.

A similar situation arises with the use of Carthage as a metaphor for Ireland, as it occurs in the final scene of

---

[29] George Steiner, *After Babel* (London: Oxford University Press, 1977). On the influence of Steiner's book on the play, see Christopher Murray, Review of *Translations*, *Irish University Review* 11.2 (Autumn 1981): 239; Richard Kearney, "Language Play: Brian Friel and Ireland's Verbal Theatre," *Studies* 62 (1983): 54-55; Dantanus, *Brian Friel*, 178; and Connolly, "Translating History," 155.

[30] Myles na gCopaleen, *An Béal Bocht* (1941), English version as Flann O'Brien, *The Poor Mouth*, trans. Patrick C. Power (London: Hart Davis, MacGibbon, 1973).

[31] On the last mentioned point, see Manus's earlier insistence to Maire that he cannot compete for the job with his own father; this reveals Hugh's story about having the job "thrust" upon him to be a fabrication. Cf. Friel, *Selected Plays*, 394, 400, 419.

Translations.[32] The play closes with overall destruction in progress, while Hugh is sitting with Maire and Jimmy, reciting more or less to himself a (simplified) passage from *The Aeneid*. This passage concerns the ancient city of Carthage which was hoped by the goddess Juno to become "the capital of all nations," while it was instead overthrown by a new race, the Romans, "kings of broad realms and proud in war" because such was the course "ordained by fate" (416-17). Since Hugh's memory fails him (although, as he says, this is a passage that he knows "backwards"), he stammers and has to start narrating all over again.

This metaphor is also quite liable to be read as an instance of mythologising the Irish past. And indeed, the ubiquitous destruction, spiritual and material, almost makes Hugh the last of the Carthaginians. The dramatic situation is again made more complex, however: Hugh is heavily inebriated, soaking wet and dishevelled, forgetting even the most basic texts he used to know by heart. Thus he perhaps should not be perceived to simply utter a timeless verity. Friel attempted once again to complicate the possibility of an unambiguous reading of a forceful image, eliminating any potential pomposity. Yet the ending of the play is so powerful that the parallel between Carthage and Gaelic Ireland comes out as a valid one, and Ireland is thus presented as a place destroyed by colonial power similar to the Roman Empire. The only alleviation of this image then lies in the fact, already mentioned, that the causes of destruction are shown to be multiple as they also include the stasis of the Gaelic order. But Hugh ultimately muses on pre-determination by fate, while his stuttering and the repetition of the lines about Carthage really makes the play point a finger in a gesture of accusation.

In contrast to this, Friel quite plainly dispels any general myths concerning the ancient and noble quality of the Irish

---

32 Frank McGuinness's play *Carthaginians* (1988) offers an interesting parallel in its use of Carthage as a metaphor for contemporary Derry; see Frank McGuinness, *Plays 1* (London: Faber, 1996) 291-379.

culture in his two later plays, *The Communication Cord* (1983) and *Making History*.[33] *The Communication Cord* condenses such a myth in the image of the "traditional" Irish thatched cottage. The cottage is repeatedly called "the centre" of everything that is really Irish. This centre is thoroughly demolished in the course of the play, first of all through the gradual revelation of how the characters abuse it (they turn the cottage respectively into a source of political power, a museum, a love nest, a commercial article or an artefact), and then also literally: in the final scene the roof falls down on the characters' heads. In *Making History*, on the other hand, the Gaelic world at the turn of the seventeenth century is shown to be a realm of petty warfare and cattle-raiding, where many Irish kings often join forces with the English to fight their Gaelic neighbours. While the main cause of such a state of affairs is undoubtedly still the English colonisation, Friel's image of the country stands in sharp contrast to the nationalist historians' version of the joint struggle of the last Irish kings against the English oppressor and their eventual flight in order to gather up an army on the Continent.

All in all, it may still be concluded that although Friel may have occasionally implied in interviews the presence of a general metanarrative behind his Field Day plays, and indeed he has been repeatedly accused of merely reformulating current metanarratives by mythologising Irish history, his plays do not allow for any consistent metanarrative to arise. Ambiguities frequently abound, while mythical and counter-mythical moments tend to stand in more or less equal balance. Moreover, individual narratives are often quite diverse, and when it appears that a metanarrative may be emerging from beyond the text, textual or dramatic irony eventually qualifies it.

The movement in Seamus Deane's early theoretical texts, on the other hand, follows an opposite direction. His intended

---

[33] Friel has repeatedly spoken of his intention to do so in *The Communication Cord*: see O'Toole, "The Man from God Knows Where," 169-70 and Comiskey, "Rehearsing Friel's New Farce," 165.

non-totalisation and openness to a plurality of micro-narratives is ironically subverted by a desire for unity, evident from both a number of contradictions present in his texts and the use of images and concepts akin to those of Irish nationalism. In relation to the discursive nature of the context within which Deane is writing, he does not particularly develop what presumably should be the next step in the approach he proposes, that is, envisaging possible patterns of mutual interaction between the revised narratives of identity. Looking at Friel's texts, on the other hand, there appears to be a significant difference again: Friel's plays not only engage with communication patterns but in fact tend to show perfect verbal communication to be impossible.

Narrative in Communication

Possessing a distinct narrative of one's own undoubtedly represents a crucial means of making sense of the world and finding one's place in it. A more effortless, though also potentially very dangerous way to establish such a guiding narrative is by subscribing to an existing metanarrative. While Friel may indeed acknowledge these options, he is also well aware of the fact that any narrative is firmly based in a broader discursive context, being inevitably created within a space defined by human interaction. And it is this interaction that becomes his particular focus: Friel is never concerned with narratives *per se*. What he examines instead are the relations between people and the position of narratives in these relations. In fact, even in a play like *Faith Healer* which consists of four extensive monologues, narrative is not the focal point; the play focuses mainly on the complex relations of the three characters, while the nature of these relations is to be glimpsed only behind the words of the story they narrate.

It is inevitable then that communication assumes a much more important role than narrative in Friel's drama, as narrative is often shown both as a product of human interaction and also as something which gains its meaning only when it enters into interaction with others. Friel's scepticism about the possibility of communicating one's feelings and mental processes through language has been well noted. Indeed, failures of communication are often the very reason for the breakdown of relationships between Friel's characters—the father-and-son relationship in *Philadelphia, Here I Come* (1964) being a famous early example—and often also for the subsequent tragic outcome. Nevertheless, attention has been paid chiefly to the verbal form of communication and its failures in Friel's drama, without really examining whether language was used merely to communicate new information or whether it perhaps also served other functions.

This is where an existing model of human communication may prove helpful, as it can provide theoretical equipment for a further analysis of Friel's approach to communication in his plays. The first general outline of the pragmatics of human interaction has resulted from the systemic approach of the Palo Alto school of psychology and psychiatry. Utilising what is essentially a psychological model in the context of contemporary Ireland, however, requires some preliminary qualifications. Its use here is not intended to imply that the nature of issues addressed in Friel's plays (and by the Field Day enterprise in general) is solely psychological. Nor is this strategy intended to serve as a comment on the causes of the present political and intercultural problems in Ireland—modern European history has most remarkably proved the realms of collective psychology to be dubious, to say the least. What the Palo Alto views do provide, however, is a plausible description of *mechanisms of interpersonal communication*, in other words of practical ways in which individuals communicate with one another, while communication between individuals inevitably stands at the basis of any communication between groups or cultures. This is also what Friel's plays are ultimately concerned with.

The Palo Alto school has made an important distinction concerning the focus of interpersonal communication. Paul Watzlawick, Janet Bavelas and Don Jackson claim in their seminal study, *Pragmatics of Human Communication*, that every communication includes two inseparable aspects, one which focuses on its content and another which centres on the relationship between the speaker and the addressee. Communication within a problematic relationship, i.e., one in which misunderstandings, conflicts of values and/or emotions exist, can reach a stage where content is almost irrelevant and the entire communication consists only in sending signals concerning the speaker's and the addressee's views of their relationship.[34] The content of communication is typically transmitted verbally. Signals about the relationship are transmitted mainly in a non-verbal manner, or through language which is not used to convey information but rather to form an analogous description of the relationship (2.53). However, the most effective way to communicate about the nature of the mutual relationship of the speaker and the addressee is verbal metacommunication, that is, explicit communication through language about the relationship (1.5, 2.33).

Watzlawick and his colleagues maintain that disorders in human communication are always connected with at least a partial loss of the ability to metacommunicate (3.55). At the same time, so-called transitional forms of communication may help to establish metacommunication, the most prominent of these being ritual. Ritual is seen as a method that can be used to translate the relational aspect of communication into verbal communication about content, thus helping to resolve problems within the relationship (3.532). Nevertheless, whenever the

34 Paul Watzlawick, Janet Beavin Bavelas and Don D. Jackson, *Pragmatics of Human Communication: A Study of Interactional Patterns, Pathologies, and Paradoxes* (New York and London: Norton, 1967)/ *Menschliche Kommunikation: Formen, Störungen, Paradoxien* (Bern und Stuttgart: Verlag Hans Huber, 1969) Section 2.3. Further references to individual sections of the book appear in parentheses in the text.

relationship suffers from a serious disorder, even such transitional forms fail. People are trapped in paradoxical communication patterns, while the obvious solution—clarifying the whole situation through verbal metacommunication—is often out of their reach. Such individuals find themselves in "double binds" where they cannot either metacommunicate or abandon their relationship, while whenever a decision has to be made, they frequently suffer from an "illusion of alternatives," i.e., a moment where none of the possible solutions can be adopted (6.43ff). The only way out of such blind alleys is to step out of the communication pattern (7.21).

When the communication patterns in Brian Friel's plays from around the Field Day period are surveyed in this light, a number of interesting observations emerge. As suggested above, *Faith Healer*, despite being the most verbal of Friel's dramas, only appears to convey its meaning by the sole content of the individual narratives. Frank, Grace and Teddy basically circle around their relationship and try to verbalise it. Each character maintains a different version of the events they have gone through together, and a different version of their attachment to one another. It is apparent that some of their statements (especially those uttered by Frank) must simply be lies, but nevertheless, as Nicholas Grene has observed, no true story can be unravelled from the monologues.[35] And that is perhaps beside the point: what seems much more important in the play, apart from the central and complex metaphor of faith healing, is the extraordinary set of relations among the three characters. One of the most remarkable aspects of the play is that despite the striking contradictions between the individual narratives the audience is able to see quite deeply into the nature of the bonds between Frank, Grace and Teddy in the end. These bonds may be viewed—in Palo Alto terminology— as defined by several double binds: Grace and Frank fight constantly but still Grace cannot leave him, Teddy suffers both

---

[35] Nicholas Grene, "Friel and Transparency," *Irish University Review* 29.1 (1999): 143.

emotionally and materially but cannot leave either Grace or Frank because of his love for them. The situation is tragically confirmed by its ultimate terminal violence. In order to disclose the nature of this complicated and paradoxical relationship, one must inevitably go beyond the words, regard language merely as an imperfect vehicle for a description of the relationship, and focus on narrative as an emotional "sketch" of what is verbally inexpressible for the characters.[36]

Faith Healer also employs the notion of ritual, which gains prominence in Friel's later works. Frank Hardy the Faith Healer is said to perform in derelict "kirks, meeting-houses or schools," places of "abandoned rituals" (332). These rituals are replaced by his show, which bears distinct features of ritual in itself. The very act of faith healing takes the form of mysterious non-verbal communication which—if successful—empowers both the healed and the healer.[37] Nevertheless, such non-verbal mystery cannot be taken as a universal cure, as the role of chance in it is only too apparent. (In fact, in most of the faith healer's sessions nothing ever happens.) Ironically, one of the most powerful moments where instinctive non-verbal understanding reaches perfection is represented by Frank's death scene: everybody knows that nothing is going to happen, and everybody knows that the situation will result in fatal violence. For Frank, this is the ultimate moment when he "renounc[es] chance [...] at long last," and the audience is brought in to share his experience by his suggestive moving downstage while speaking his final lines (376). This scene in

[36] Interestingly, a metaphorical comment is made along similar lines early in the play in the emblematic image of Miss Mulatto and her pigeons. One day, Teddy asks Miss Mulatto, a woman who is all "smothered" by her pigeons when she starts talking to them in what seems to be their language about what it was that she actually said to them. "Say to them? How would I know what I say to them, Teddy? I just make sounds at them," retorts the woman, and Teddy simply cannot accept such an answer. To him, she just "speaks pigeon" and asks the pigeons to perform with her, while in fact her "pigeon words" only indicate affection and are entirely devoid of content. Brian Friel, *Faith Healer, Selected Plays*, 356. Further references appear in parentheses in the text.

[37] Cf. Grene, "Friel and Transparency," 144.

fact appears as the climax of a "Bacchanalian night" which is described as a particular kind of ritual, perhaps one of homecoming and hospitality. The ritual gets however "consciously and relentlessly debauched" (340). And the price for such violation is high.

Translations continues to explore the role of language in human interaction. This time the problem is approached from a different angle, as problematic communication shifts from a personal level to that of two different cultural contexts. Friel's scepticism about verbal communication becomes much more overt here. Even in instances where two people from different contexts happen to speak the same language, it is almost impossible for them to understand their respective feelings. Paradoxically, it is only in the love-scene between Maire and Yolland, who do not speak the same language, that perfect communication about their mutual affection and spiritual unity takes place. Moreover, this emotional understanding brings them to utter almost exactly the same words—apart from the ironic moment when Yolland expresses his desire to stay with Maire in Ballybeg, while Maire is determined to leave with him for England; but even here their unanimous insistence on staying together is clear (426-30).

There are two instances in the play of scepticism concerning the role of language in human understanding being explicitly stated. The first is epitomised by the moment when Yolland expresses his wish to learn Irish. He almost immediately muses:

Even if I did speak Irish I'd always be an outsider here, wouldn't I? I may learn the password but the language of the tribe will always elude me, won't it? The private core will always be ... hermetic, won't it? [416]

A confirmation of this view is eventually provided also from the perspective of the local Irish. Hugh tells Maire at the end of the play:

Yes, I will teach you English, Maire Chatach. [...] But don't expect too much. I will provide you with the available words and the available grammar. But will that help you to interpret between privacies? I have no idea. But it's all we have. I have no idea at all. [446]

There is nothing in the play to justify any greater measure of optimism on this issue. Despite this, an observation made by numerous commentators should be remembered: the play itself ironically communicates chiefly through its language, and it is the English language at that.

The very title of Friel's subsequent play, *The Communication Cord*, indicates one of its central concerns: issues of communication are again explicitly addressed and further developed. Right at the beginning of the play, Tim introduces his linguistic theory, which is in fact only a version of a simplistic analytical theory of communication. According to this theory, communication is considered to be merely a matter of language: once the speaker and the addressee share the same code, and assuming that there is no external interference, perfect communication can be established. In fact, Owen in *Translations* seems initially to share this view, as his response to Yolland's scepticism about the chances of an outsider being able to understand the Irish is "You can learn to decode us" (416).

Tim's theory is completely demolished in *The Communication Cord*. This is achieved in various ways. First of all, the play points out the difficulties inherent in establishing the same code even in situations where people have a common language, for example, English. Many words or utterances are often interpreted as having a meaning significantly different from that intended, thus documenting a whole set of problems concerning verbal communication. One of the earliest and also most remarkable examples is provided by the comedy of Tim interpreting Jack's repetitive question about the nature of his thesis as a sign of Jack's interest, while exactly the opposite is clearly true.[38] Moreover, individual words, phrases and even "response cries" keep on changing their meaning according to the context in which they are uttered. These contexts radically alter in the course of a few minutes, as characters either adopt or are forced into various kinds of role-playing, in line with the farcical nature of the action which has people appearing on the stage at exactly the wrong moment.

The final demise of Tim's theory again takes an explicit form. In an enamoured conversation, Claire and Tim correctly point out the subordinate role that language plays whenever communication concerns close personal relationships, as the primary focus is often not on the content of the words at all:

> TIM: [...] I'm not too sure what I'm saying.
> CLAIRE: I don't know what you're saying either but I think I know what's implicit in it.
> [...]
> TIM: Even if what I'm saying is rubbish?
> CLAIRE: Yes.
> TIM: Like "this is our first cathedral"?
> CLAIRE: Like that.
> TIM: Like "this is the true centre"?
> CLAIRE: I think I know what's implicit in that.
> TIM: Maybe the message doesn't matter at all then. [85]

The eventual literal collapse of the scene when the roof of the house caves in then clearly parallels the fate of Tim's original views on communication.

Dancing at Lughnasa (1990) in effect marks Friel's departure from the Field Day Theatre Company. It is also a play in which the inquiry into various versions of the Irish past is pushed into the background, as Friel for the most part presents a—by then—fairly standard image of conservative, impoverished 1930s Ireland oppressed by the dogmas of the Catholic Church and by the version of collective identity maintained by the state.

---

[38] Brian Friel, *The Communication Cord* (London and Boston: Faber, 1983) 19. Further references appear in parentheses in the text.

At the same time, *Dancing at Lughnasa* continues to explore various forms of human interaction, developing an alternative focus on dance and ritual.

The very first dance of Chris and Gerry provides a brilliant example of dance serving as a "transitional" form of communication. Before the couple dance, their conversation is really awkward. Their dance is initially accompanied only by Gerry singing the tune of "Dancing in the Dark"—without the words—but in a short space of time, dancing results in metacommunication about their relationship:

> GERRY: [...] Marry me, Chrissie. (*Pause.*) Are you listening to me?
> CHRIS: I hear you.
> GERRY: Will you marry me when I come back in two weeks?
> CHRIS: I don't think so, Gerry.
> GERRY: I'm mad about you. You know I am. I've always been mad about you.
> CHRIS: When you're with me.
> GERRY: Leave this house and come away with–
> CHRIS: But you'd walk out on me again. You wouldn't intend to but that's what would happen because that's your nature and you can't help yourself.[39]

This metacommunication succeeds in bringing about a brief period of happiness for Chris (and perhaps Gerry as well?). However, it seems that the only time when Chris and Gerry achieve perfect communication and mutual understanding is when they dance, even when they do so in complete silence. This is the case with their final dance, described by Michael as a marriage ritual (42). The "ceremony" is ironically qualified later on in the play though, as Michael reveals that his father was already married to someone else at the time (61).

But the terms "dance" and "ritual" are multifaceted in *Dancing at Lughnasa* and defy hypostatisation. Not only are

---

[39] Brian Friel, *Dancing at Lughnasa* (London and Boston: Faber, 1990) 33. Further references appear in parentheses in the text.

there different dances and rituals performed or described: all of them also serve different functions with the individual characters. Most remarkably, there is a significant contrast between the role of ritual and dance in the primitive society[40] of Ryanga (as described by Jack) and in the 1930s Ireland of the play. In Ryanga, periodical rituals and dances which form their part are firmly embedded in the social order and serve to confirm this order, while providing, for instance, collective purification.

This is radically different in Ballybeg. Although collective rituals are still performed at Lughnasa, they are clearly shown as something marginalised and not recognised by society. The Lughnasa rituals are depicted as wild, inebriated celebrations which may even result in tragedy, as demonstrated by young Sweeney's serious burns following a fall into the fire (16ff). These rituals have no major impact on the community, however. The individual initiation rite of Rose, the completion of which she announces by bringing in her dead pet rooster and laying it in the centre of the improvised picnic ground, also lacks any connectedness with the larger social context and is perceived more as a tragic gesture (67ff). Finally, the fact that ritual cannot be either hypostatised or indeed taken as a functional remedy for the community is further stressed by the fact that the term appears to have an extremely broad application, being used by Jack to describe even the annual picking of bilberries with his mother (46).

The function of the individual dances performed by the characters also varies. In a remarkable scene in Act I which has all the women in the house dancing vigorously to traditional music on the radio, dance is used to alleviate rage and frustration, and break the stifling situation in which the sisters live. The dancers themselves are nonetheless aware of the limited impact of their dance, as they perform it partially as a parody (21-22). A different kind of dance may serve to achieve

---

[40] The term "primitive" is used here in the sense customary in anthropology since Claude Lévi-Strauss.

momentary harmony and help two people to communicate their mutual affection perfectly, as suggested above with Chris and Gerry. But again, this moment of unity is only temporary; indeed, one could speak of a moment of perfect union before a final break-up (Gerry never comes back again after his time in Spain). Maggie in fact describes a very similar moment when remembering the beautiful dance of her friend Bernie O'Donnell with a man called Brian McGuinness and their unity in it, while Brian left for Australia shortly afterwards (20). Again, dance can be hardly taken as a long-term "cure" of human relationships or indeed of the societal structures. Characters are shown to be trapped in a rather hopeless and enclosed social context, and while dancing or performing rituals may perhaps provide them with momentary relief, they soon find themselves back in the same plight. Eventually, the whole family in the play dissolves.

Despite this, *Dancing at Lughnasa* may appear to conclude with a demise of verbal communication. In his last monologue, Michael seems to express extreme scepticism regarding the role of words in human interaction and in life in general and to prefer dance as a kind of ritual that is the only way to convey the meaning of his memories:

> When I remember it, I think of it as dancing. Dancing with eyes half closed because to open them up would break the spell. Dancing as if language had surrendered to movement—as if this ritual, this wordless ceremony, was now the way to speak, to whisper private and sacred things, to be in touch with some otherness. Dancing as if the very heart of life and all its hopes might be found in those assuaging notes and those hushed rhythms and in those silent and hypnotic movements. Dancing as if language no longer existed because words were no longer necessary. [71]

As Anna McMullan and Nicholas Grene have both pointed out,[41] there is an apparent irony about the whole monologue, as the ostensible dismissal of language is itself firmly embedded in language—and one of Friel's most poetic passages at that— while the whole play is framed by Michael's narrative and presented consistently as a story with the one narrator. Language thus seems to be paradoxically confirmed as still the most powerful means of commenting on human relationships, despite the fact that it frequently provides no help at all. This view is also reinforced by the very limited effect of transitional or non-verbal forms of communication in the play. On the whole, only brief moments of perfect communication about problematic relationships can be achieved, and even the final enchanting image conjured up by Michael's words is quite akin to the moments when the characters dance, the moments when once you open your eyes, the spell is broken, but, even so, open them is what you eventually must do.

Conflicts within the Fifth Province

One of my initial comments on Lyotard's vision of a world consisting solely of particular micro-narratives concerned the fact that as far as the practical means of achieving such a world are concerned, Lyotard offered little assistance. Indeed, a closer analysis of the basic ideas formulated by Field Day distinctly reveals how difficult it is to effect a transfer from a world dominated by existing metanarratives. It seems that any collective effort setting out to effect such a change, particularly one operating in a largely polarised context such as Northern Ireland, is bound to create some form of a metanarrative of its own. This metanarrative does not necessarily have to aim for dominance: it may operate merely as a metanarrative of transfer. The underlying desire for unity inherent in Field Day

---

[41] Anna McMullan, "'In touch with some otherness': Gender, Authority and the Body in Dancing at Lughnasa," *Irish University Review* 29.1 (1999): 99; Grene, "Friel and Transparency," 141-42.

concepts like the "fifth province" however points out its affinity with previous grand narratives such as that of the national revival. It should be stressed, however, that unlike the metanarrative of cultural and political resurgence which guided the early national theatre—and the Literary Revival *per se*— Field Day have been sparsely seen to perform hegemonic actions. These have been limited almost solely to the controversial demarcation of the territory encompassed by *The Field Day Anthology of Irish Writing* (although the use of the term "hegemonic" in this context may be only partially appropriate—see the discussion above) and the rejection of David Rudkin's play *The Saxon Shore* (1983) and Frank McGuinness's *Observe the Sons of Ulster Marching towards the Somme* (1984). As Shaun Richards has suggested, both plays may have been rejected on technical or procedural grounds but one suspects that it was most probably their political focus on "the Protestant predicament" that was objectionable to the Field Day directors.[42]

Richards has also aptly noted that Field Day's propensity to regard the situation in Northern Ireland as essentially colonial implied that its politics equalled that of non-sectarian republicanism.[43] It is hardly surprising then that many scholars and commentators with a Unionist background have perceived the politics of the enterprise as an acute problem. Edna Longley in particular has offered searing critical observations focused on Field Day's self-justifications, making similar comments to Richards about the fundamental nationalist bias of post-colonial approaches to the situation in Ireland, and claiming that Field Day thus at times "simply translate[d] traditional concepts into an updated idiom."[44]

---

[42] Shaun Richards, "Field Day's Fifth Province: Avenue or Impasse?" *Culture and Politics in Northern Ireland, 1960-1990*, ed. Eamonn Hughes (Buckingham and Bristol, PA: Open University Press, 1991) 142-43.

[43] Richards, "Field Day's Fifth Province?" 140, 142.

[44] Longley, *From Cathleen to Anorexia*, 12-13. See also note 13 above.

All this does not necessarily mean though that Field Day's effort to dismantle metanarratives has been worthless or counterproductive: in principle, there seems indeed no other way to plausibly contribute to the destabilising of entrenched positions on Irish history and culture. Field Day have on the other hand only demonstrated again that Lyotard's vision is really a utopia. A world consisting solely of interacting micro-narratives could perhaps be accomplished in an environment defined by the non-existence of conflicting metanarratives or even differences of opinion. Sadly, contemporary Northern Ireland provides only a most blatant counter-example of such an environment.

Despite all the failings of its theoretical position within what Edna Longley has termed a general "ideological rigor mortis,"[45] the Field Day enterprise has achieved major success in terms of actual practice. The Field Day Theatre Company undoubtedly enlivened Irish theatre, while several landmarks of modern drama were created within its framework. A similar revitalisation may be perceived in the area of scholarly writing through the publication of a number of Field Day essays and monographs, together with the formidable anthology of Irish literature which made available an incredible amount of material that had often been hard to access.

The difficulties inherent in any attempt to redefine the discursive context in Ireland have been confirmed by Brian Friel's plays which have gradually shifted from reviewing existing metanarratives and replacing them by individual stories—while at times arguably embodying traces of other underlying myths—to a detailed examination of human communication and its role in individual relationships. The scepticism Friel's plays gradually come to express about communication concerns both its verbal and non-verbal forms within problematic contexts of interaction. However, pessimistic as the plays may be about the chances one has of stepping out of rigid interactive patterns, the very description

45 Longley, *From Cathleen to Anorexia*, 22.

of these patterns and their communication to the audience within powerful dramas testify to Friel's significance not only as a leading playwright but also a sharp cultural commentator.

"Comedy of Terrors": Stewart Parker

Surveying the drama of Ireland over four decades, Stewart Parker (1941-1988) represents a unique experimental voice. In a lecture delivered in 1981, Parker himself has indeed noted that

> two kinds of playwriting [...] have been conspicuous by their absence in Ireland—experimentalism, and politically committed work (in the socialist sense). [I cannot help] assailing yet again the profound suspicion of ideas in Irish culture, its conservatism, its self-satisfied provincialism.[1]

Regarding the tradition of Irish drama which has so far been defined chiefly by the Abbey Theatre as exhausted and no longer relevant, Parker went on to say: "the Irish playwright today—or certainly the Northern Irish playwright—has to invent the theatre all over again, and conjure out of thin air (or rather out of thick and acrid air) a place within it for himself."[2]

Parker's views and concerns were very much defined by the fact that he perceived himself as a Belfast playwright, even more so after returning home from a teaching post in the US shortly after the eruption of the "Troubles," feeling that this was his duty to his native Northern Ireland. His work was defined throughout by a wonderful inventiveness both regarding the subject and the dramatic form, accompanied by active engagement with the politics of the violent conflict in the

---

[1] Stewart Parker, "State of Play," *The Canadian Journal of Irish Studies* 7.1 (June 1981): 8.

[2] Parker, "State of Play," 9.

North and possible solutions to this conflict. Parker claimed that as the politicians were "visionless almost to a man" and possessed by sectarianism, it fell to the artists to "construct a working model of wholeness by means of which this society can begin to hold up its head in the world."[3] In order to do so, however, art was not to turn into propaganda if it were to be of any long-term use, as agit-prop "defeats its own ends by preaching only to the converted," while "the rest of the audience is alienated and switches off."[4] Parker hence insisted, in tune with this comment that rings absolutely true:

> I see no point in writing a "plea" for unity between prods and taigs. What use has piety been? I can only see a point in actually embodying that unity, practising that inclusiveness, in an artistic image; creating it as an act of the imagination, postulating it before an audience.[5]

Given Parker's approach, it is not surprising that his last play, *Pentecost*, received a production from the Field Day Theatre Company, with whom it came to share some basic aesthetic principles. But as it will become apparent, *Pentecost* is really the odd one out among Parker's dramas due to its resistance to irony as a central structuring device. The following pages aim to present a reading of Parker's views on modern theatre and Ireland/Northern Ireland against his actual theatrical practice, culminating in a discussion of *Pentecost* in this light.

The invention of the new drama for Northern Ireland implied for Parker that theatre should become essentially ludic, constantly innovating itself in order to capture the unsettled and unsettling contemporary reality, while also suggesting where changes could be effected in the society: "The drama constantly demands that we reinvent it, that we transform it

[3] Stewart Parker, *Dramatis Personae*, John Malone Memorial Lecture (Belfast: Queen's University, 1986) 19.
[4] Parker, *Dramatis Personae*, 8.
[5] Quoted in John Fairleigh, ed., *Stewart Parker*. Supplement to *Fortnight* 278 (Nov. 1989): ii.

with new ways of showing, to cater adequately to the unique plight in which we find ourselves."[6] The playwright claimed that theatre:

> can contain the conflicts and contradictions, the cruelty and the killings, the implacable ghosts, the unending rancour, pettiness and meanness of spirit, the poverty of imagination and evasion of truth which unites our two communities in their compact of mutual impotence and sterility[...] it can demonstrate and celebrate a language as wholesome and nutritious as a wheaten farl, a stony wit and devious humour, an experiential vivacity and wholeheartedness, a true instinct for hospitality and generosity, which also and equally unite our two communities.[7]

In order to facilitate true insight into the state of affairs in the province, the playwright has to combine in a Brechtian way an element of instruction with an element of entertainment,[8] and couch these in incessant experimentation. The need for experiment was summed up by Parker in his notion of play, a concept central to his aesthetic. Parker came to conceptualise play after having read the influential study of the human play impulse, Johan Huizinga's *Homo Ludens*: "Play is how we experiment, imagine, invent, and move forward. Play is above all how we enjoy the earth and celebrate our life upon it."[9]

Parker delivered the John Malone memorial lecture articulating his creative principles in detail in 1986 (its title—"Dramatis Personae"—being an echo of Yeats, with a touch of self-irony). Incidentally, it was in the same year that Jean-François Lyotard wrote about the conflict between nostalgia and experiment as a determining moment for art and thought in the modern era. When speaking about the two attitudes that

6 Parker, *Dramatis Personae*, 20.
7 Parker, *Dramatis Personae*, 19.
8 The influence of Brecht on Parker may be judged by the fact that at least one third of Parker's John Malone lecture is devoted to Brecht's ideas on theatre and politics.
9 Parker, *Dramatis Personae*, 8.

may be adopted towards the sublime discrepancy between the presentable and the thinkable—one that defines the nature of modernity—Lyotard characterised the approach of the experimental, innovative artist as one that centres on "the power of the faculty to conceive [...] and on the extension of being and jubilation which come from inventing new rules of the game" of the arts.[10] This indeed seems to be quite a fitting description of Parker's dramatic practice: Parker constantly changes his method, blends different techniques according to what his material requires, and, above all, his plays radiate precisely the kind of joy that springs from "inventing new rules of the game."

There are further links to be highlighted regarding the play principle. Elmer Andrews has pointed out that Parker's play functions as a means of transcendence of the flawed contemporary reality: play according to Andrews "is a kind of semiotic force which interrogates and disrupts given identities, stable meanings and institutions, with a view to producing a new human subject." In the playwright's imaginative inventiveness Andrews senses a note of "an old-fashioned Romantic humanism," albeit not one that would enthrone imagination "as a comfortingly absolute alternative to history."[11]

Andrews's association of play with transcendence in Parker seems to be quite convincing. However, there is a more direct link to Romanticism and the German originator of the concept of Romantic irony, Friedrich Schlegel. For Schlegel, irony springs from an awareness of the chaos and corruption of the

---

10 Jean-François Lyotard, *Le postmoderne expliqué aux enfants* (Paris: Editions Galilée, 1986) 30. English quotation from Jean-François Lyotard, *The Postmodern Explained to Children*, trans. Julian Pefanis, Morgan Thomas, et al. (London: Turnaround, 1992) 22.

11 Elmer Andrews, "The Will to Freedom: Politics and Play in the Theatre of Stewart Parker," *Irish Writers and Politics*, eds. Okifumi Komesu and Masaru Sekine (Gerrards Cross: Colin Smythe, 1989) 239.

world, and it serves as a mode of reflection on its condition.[12] The awareness of chaos, however, is not simply negative in Schlegel's view, as chaos is "only such a confusion, out of which a world can arise,"[13] or more specifically, chaos in itself entails the potential to develop into a new Golden Age.[14] Irony thus acts as an instrument of transcendence. It is at the same time essentially connected with creativity and gives a paradoxical expression to the hope for a new uncorrupted era. Paradoxicality is fundamentally attached to reflective irony for Schlegel: indeed, it is its "conditio sine qua non."[15] The yearning for another Golden Age in effect amounts to a utopian desire. And Parker's work has much in common with Schlegel's fragments: his plays are playful, ironic and vastly entertaining dramatisations of paradoxes radiating a difficult yearning.

The association of Parker's dramatic principle with Schlegel's philosophical and aesthetic mode of reflection thus reveals a strong tie between play and irony. A similar connection, and one also very relevant to Parker's drama, is apparent in Jacques Derrida's idea of deconstruction. In a broad sense, Derrida's notion of play may be viewed as an ironic articulation of paradoxicality. Moreover, his brand of play embraces the paradoxes, affirming them "in a certain laughter and a certain step of the dance," to use Derrida's words.[16] For this reason, Derrida hails the non-hegemonic creativity of the

---

[12] "Ironie ist klares Bewußtsein der ewigen Agilität, des unendlich vollen Chaos." (Irony is clear consciousness of eternal mobility, of the infinite fullness of chaos.) Friedrich Schlegel, *Ideen*, No. 69, *Charakteristiken und Kritiken I (1796-1801)*, hrsg. Hans Eichner (München: Verlag Ferd. Schöningh/ Zürich: Thomas Verlag, 1967) 263. English translation by Lilian R. Furst, *Fictions of Romantic Irony in European Narrative, 1760-1857* (London: Macmillan, 1984) 27.

[13] "Nur diejenige Verworrenheit ist ein Chaos, aus der eine Welt entspringen kann." Schlegel, *Ideen*, No. 71, 263. My translation.

[14] Ralf Schnell, *Die verkehrte Welt. Literarische Ironie im 19. Jahrhundert* (Stuttgart: J.B. Metzlersche Verlagsbuchhandlung, 1989) 4.

[15] Friedrich Schlegel, *Literary Notebooks 1797-1801*, No. 1068, quoted in Furst, *Fictions of Romantic Irony*, 27, 242n.

[16] Jacques Derrida, "Différance," *Margins of Philosophy*, trans. Alan Bass (Brighton: Harvester, 1982) 27.

bricoleur who is aware that his/her construction is being constantly dismantled by the very nature of its material.[17] The play of deconstruction emphatically does not serve as a means of transcendence in the metaphysical sense; nonetheless, it is similar to Parker's play in the sense of transcending the established stereotypical and/or hegemonic meanings and institutions with the aim of dismantling them.

There is, admittedly, a difference in that Derrida never strives for the accomplishment of a new unity. Parker's leaning is, on the other hand, clearly towards the creation of both aesthetic and social unity, as noted above. In addition to this, his plays are also directed at a reconstitution of the individual selves of his protagonists (however overstated Andrews's assertion about the creation of "a new human subject" may seem in the light of the playwright's irony). Despite such aspirations, Parker's actual dramatic practice brings the principle of play very close to Derrida's, as of all of his stage plays it is only *Pentecost* that actually offers a vision of "wholeness."

Irony has a ubiquitous presence in Parker's drama. His mechanics of play are, however, always deeply embedded in an essentially mimetic enterprise: as noted earlier, the plays strive to offer reflections and comments on contemporary Ireland, in particular the violent impasse in the North. What should be examined, therefore, is how Parker's principle of play operates within his ever-changing mimetic strategy, focusing on the mimetic modes utilised in the most important of his plays: *Spokesong* (1975) and the "Three Plays for Ireland" (published in 1989). Particular attention should also be paid to the deployment of the principal motif of ghosts which stands out as Parker's key figurative structure.

---

17 Cf. Jacques Derrida, "Structure, Sign and Play in the Discourse of the Humanities," *Writing and Difference*, trans. Alan Bass (London: Routledge and Kegan Paul, 1978) 278-94.

"All plays are ghost plays," Parker asserted in his Belfast lecture.[18] His use of ghosts, however, is subject to the same kind of ongoing modification as the overall strategy itself, and the trajectory of spectral transformations forms an important line in the playwright's creative effort as a whole. Spectral characters already appear in Parker's first play to be staged, *Spokesong*,[19] only to re-emerge in the final triptych of history plays concerned with "three self-contained groups of figures, from the eighteenth, nineteenth and twentieth centuries respectively, hinged together in a continuing comedy of terrors."[20] By then, spectres and wraiths had become so central that Parker devoted a considerable part of his brief preface to them:

Ancestral voices prophesy and bicker, and the ghosts of your own time and birthplace wrestle and dance, in any play you choose to write—but most obviously when it actually is a history play. [...] Plays and ghosts have a lot in common. The energy which flows from some intense moment of conflict in a particular time and place seems to activate them both. Plays intend to achieve resolution, however, whilst ghosts appear to be stuck fast in the quest for vengeance. Ghosts are uncompleted souls. [9]

The playwright's predicament in Northern Ireland—according to Parker—consists in the compulsion to incessantly struggle with the past embodied in spectral shapes. Parker's drama makes two essential points about these ghosts: it is virtually impossible to wrestle free from the influence of one's "ancestral wraiths" (9) while any kind of harmonious future may be achieved only once the ghostly voices have been laid to rest.[21]

---

18 Parker, *Dramatis Personae*, 18.
19 Preceded by *The Iceberg* (1975), a radio play narrated by the ghosts of two Belfast shipyard workers on board the *Titanic*.
20 Stewart Parker, Introduction to *Three Plays for Ireland* (London: Oberon Books, 1989) 9. Further references to the introduction and plays in this edition appear in parentheses in the text.
21 Parker's call for exorcism stands in sharp contrast to Padraic Pearse's image of Ireland as a country shaped by ghosts where the only way to "appease a ghost"

Being based on conflict, drama provides a perfect vehicle for the exorcism of wrestling ghosts. Indeed, as a playwright, Parker in turn relished the potential offered by his ghost-ridden province, saying that "the most satisfying drama occurs when two characters wrestle each other to a draw."[22] The ghosts of the past are to be fought; but as they cannot be subdued entirely (after all, they still form an essential ingredient of individual identity), it is truce and reconciliation that is the desired outcome of the fight.

Spokesong forms a preamble of a kind to the three later plays as regards the placation of ghosts. Set in contemporary Belfast "and the eighty years preceding,"[23] it directly depicts the grim reality of the Troubles (as does *Pentecost*) and combines this with retrospects of the characters' past (similarly to *Pratt's Fall*, *Northern Star* or *Heavenly Bodies*). Apart from the juxtaposition of the past—which is re-presented on the stage—and the present, the mimetic strategy of *Spokesong* consists in a playful blending of several dramatic genres. "Realism is only one mode among several adopted during the action" (3) is Parker's comment in an opening stage direction; the other modes include circus performance, variety and music-hall, mime and farce. Moreover, Parker employs elements of pastiche also in the play's language, most remarkably when endowing the nationalist, emancipated beauty, Kitty, with utterances in the style of Oscar Wilde.[24]

There is an overall stress on circularity (reminiscent of another Irish masterpiece featuring bicycles, Flann O'Brien's

---

is to "do the thing it asks you" at whatever cost. Cf. Padraic H. Pearse, Preface to "Ghosts" (1915), *Collected Works of Pádraic H. Pearse: Political Writings and Speeches* (Dublin: Phoenix, 1924) 221.

[22] Quoted in Lynne Parker, "Wrestling with Flesh and Blood," Fairleigh, *Stewart Parker*, vii.

[23] Stewart Parker, *Plays: 1* (London: Methuen, 2000) 3. Further references appear in parentheses in the text.

[24] Daisy, the young woman who eventually plays the same role for Frank as Kitty did for his grandfather, finally matches her in the delightful quip "Is that *my* bicycle frame you are wearing?" (74).

The Third Policeman): the wheel is a key image, embodied in the centrality of the bicycle, which later develops within a somewhat jeering pun that extends the "common wheel" into the "common weal" (67-68). The stage represents a bike shop where family history is replayed, while individual characters frantically cycle around the crammed space. Finally, family history seems also about to be re-enacted with a slight variation when Frank and Daisy virtually step into Frank's grandparents' shoes and are all set to continue running the bike shop (while the "evil" brother Julian robs the till again; 74). Their enterprise is not merely eccentric like that of the grandparents: it seems patently absurd, as bombs are exploding everywhere around and the house is destined for demolition. In spite of this, the whole play provides an exuberant celebration of vitality and humour in the face of fatal circumstances, and the repetition of family history is presented as the climax of this paradoxical celebration. There is joy on the stage and joy in the audience, albeit—on further reflection—with a chill in the spine.[25]

As it is partly a memory play, *Spokesong* features its own dose of spectres, the two central ones being the ghosts of Frank's grandparents. Francis and Kitty serve as the main protagonists in all the scenes from Frank's personal history. At the end of the play, they are not quite "laid to rest": after going somewhat berserk in their claims about the universal utility of the bicycle, the lights are switched off on them through an hyperbolical act of magic performed by a drunken Frank and the Trick Cyclist, a shape-changing character intended by Parker to represent "the spirit of Belfast" (70-71).[26] However, what may initially seem a rather unorthodox act of exorcism is

---

[25] Speaking about Brecht in his John Malone lecture, Parker took considerable pains to also stress the—rather arguable—ubiquity of humour in the German's work. The other master playwright chosen by Parker for celebration in this context was, significantly, Beckett. See Parker, *Dramatic Personae*, 10, 14-17.

[26] Quoted in Marilynn Richtarik, "'Ireland, the Continuous Past': Stewart Parker's Belfast History Plays," *A Century of Irish Drama: Widening the Stage*, eds. Stephen Watt, Eileen Morgan and Shakir Mustafa (Bloomington and Indianapolis: Indiana University Press, 2000) 262.

ironically undermined by Frank and Daisy's adoption of roles analogous to their predecessors. Although Francis and Kitty may not be a particularly dangerous species of ghosts, they may rise from their "bed" (70) at any time.

All in all, the play reflects well its author's intention to write about contemporaneous Belfast in its complexity "in such a way that the audience would be taken completely by surprise, caught without its preconceptions." This meant, for instance, writing "a play about the history of the bicycle—because that is the most unlikely way in the world to get into the subject of Northern Ireland."[27]

Northern Star (1984) is a ghost play in a sense similar to *Spokesong*, as most of its action consists in Henry Joy McCracken replaying scenes from the 1798 rising of the United Irishmen and communicating with the past selves of his fellow insurgents. The play's mimetic strategy again combines retrospective with the events of one night in a ruined country cottage, and eventually with the future scene of McCracken's unheroic execution.

Parker's *Northern Star* is essentially a tragedy. Within its tragic framework, however, it again involves an extensive mixture of genres, for the individual stages of the rising are cast in the style of a number of prominent Irish playwrights from Farquhar to Behan and Beckett. Parker himself referred to his strategy as that of pastiche (10), substantially developing a technique employed in the earlier *Spokesong*. The framing narrative of McCracken in the derelict cottage, together with the account of the Rebellion presented through the individual dramatic styles provide ironic detachment from the events and ideas, and exhibit a degree of their ironic transcendence. However, this detachment cannot free McCracken from the trap of history, and when faced with the ultimate choice between abandoning his idea of a united Ireland and emigrating, or facing death, McCracken opts for the latter. His half-desperate, half-mocking attempt to at least deliver a memorable speech

---

[27] Quoted in Richtarik, "'Ireland, the Continuous Past,'" 261.

from under the gallows is drowned by the angry, malicious sound of a lambeg drum (76). Here Parker deliberately replaces the noise of the stamping horses that silenced the words of the historical Henry Joy McCracken with the thunder of the symbolic Unionist drum, pointing out the Protestants' lack of hope for harmonious coexistence under the influence of militant Unionism.[28]

The play also introduces a ghost of a different order: the Phantom Bride. The Bride is presented as a figure of local lore, the spectre of a young woman engaged to the local free-thinker O'Keefe who began building the cottage now being used by McCracken as a hiding place, and who in all probability had been murdered by his neighbours. The woman's ghost acquires distinctly allegorical features in the play: the Phantom Bride kills the English captain about to arrest McCracken and transforms herself into a Woman of Ireland figure, an allegorical lover who takes McCracken away from his real lover, Mary Bodle and their baby. Significantly, the Phantom Bride performs her "predatory leap" on McCracken at the moment when he re-enacts on the stage taking his oath of allegiance to the United Irishmen. The first half closes with the spectre's bare legs clamped around McCracken's waist: he is both symbolically and sexually united with and devoured by a vampiric, voracious version of Cathleen ni Houlihan (49-50). The spectral lover never reappears in the play, while being far from having been put to rest—according to the play's logic, she may well be still guarding the door of the symbolic ruined house.

Needless to say, the association of the allegorical female with McCracken and his Protestant associates is quite

---

28 The execution is discussed by Akiko Satake in her article "The Seven Ages of Harry Joy McCracken: Stewart Parker's Northern Star as a History Play of the United Irishmen in 1798," *Theatre Stuff: Critical Essays on Contemporary Irish Theatre*, ed. Eamonn Jordan (Dublin: Carysfort Press, 2000) 177. Cf. also Richtarik, "'Ireland, the Continuous Past,'" 268.

provocative. Marilynn Richtarik sums up the political message succinctly:

> Incredibly, given the political context of Parker's own lifetime […], these founders of Irish republicanism [i.e., the radical leaders of the United Irishmen] were also, in the main, Presbyterians. In putting them at the heart of his drama, Parker was sending a direct message to his fellow Northern Protestants that, deny it though they might, they had a republican heritage. By placing the likes of McCracken at centre stage, Parker was also signalling his dissatisfaction with the version of Irish history that had written Protestants out of the story of the nation.[29]

The subversion of Catholic nationalism thus complements the rejection of radical Unionism in the play.

Northern Star is also Parker's first play to explicitly introduce the motif of Belfast as a ghost town. Belfast is already thematised in *Spokesong*: there it is described alternately as "a slab of granite" (57), as "poison" (58) and as "a brutal hole" (58). However, the negative image of the place is balanced in *Spokesong* by its depiction both as an inherent part of Frank's self ("It *is* you." 58), and, at the same time, an organism in need of curing (6), while the play closes with a joyous celebration of life—in Belfast. *Northern Star* offers nothing of the sort: the place remains a half-built, half-destroyed dwelling haunted by ghosts, despite the affection still felt for it by some of its inhabitants. "It's a ghost town now and always will be," concludes Parker's McCracken, a realm of "angry and implacable ghosts. Me condemned to be one of their number" (75). No magical dispatch of ghosts to eternal slumber happens this time.

Parker's play about the United Irishmen, together with his stylistic experimentation in general, makes an interesting parallel with Denis Johnston's much earlier avant-garde

---

29 Richtarik, "'Ireland, the Continuous Past,'" 265.

innovations in *The Old Lady Says "No!"*[30] The list of similar motives could certainly begin with the lascivious vampire Cathleen ni Houlihan who despite her nature does not receive merely negative treatment in either of the plays. While Johnston's parodic figure helps to deliver scathing social critique, Parker's spectre is seen to save McCracken's life in *Northern Star*, though arguably in order to preserve him for herself only (49). Even more prominently, Johnston's double-edged depiction of Dublin finds a fitting analogy in Parker's Belfast of *Northern Star*, summarised in the remarkable ambivalent final speech of the respective central characters.[31] But while Johnston's "strumpet city" of the dancing shadows receives pardon, Parker's "pain-obsessed cripple" of a town (75) must wait until *Pentecost* to reach the stage of complete exorcism.

Heavenly Bodies (1986), the next play in the triptych of "plays for Ireland," shifts the focus to the position of the artist within the tensions created by the claims of the nationalists on the one hand and the lure of the English stage on the other, together with commercial pressures and the tastes of audiences. The play centres around the figure of Dion Boucicault, probably the most popular dramatist of Victorian Britain and a prominent representative of the long line of Irish playwrights who left Ireland to make their fame in London. Parker called the method of this play "a kind of collage" (10). *Heavenly Bodies* again consists of a framing situation delineated by Boucicault's conversation with his "Mephistophelean sparring partner" (9), Johnny Patterson, the ghost of a murdered Irish clown and author of popular tunes such as "The Garden Where the Praities Grow" or "The Hat my Father Wore," notoriously appropriated later as "The Sash" of Orangeism (10). Patterson arrives on the scene in order to transport Boucicault's soul to the afterlife. The central question in the play is whether the

---

[30] This has been noted also by Nicholas Grene: cf. Grene, *The Politics of Irish Drama*, 167.

[31] For a sketch of the juxtaposition, see Satake, "The Seven Ages," 184.

cunning playwright deserves a place in Heaven or is to be forfeited to Satan, or even worse, be condemned to eternal oblivion in limbo.

The framing situation is interlaced by segments that replay the story of Boucicault's life, together with a selection of significant scenes from his plays. The style of these scenes radically alters (although the changes are fewer in comparison with the rather overloaded *Northern Star*); this time, Parker chiefly replicates the actual shift in Boucicault's writing from comedy of manners to melodrama, and needs only to cast particular scenes from the playwright's life in the style relevant for his plays at the given period. An ironic intent is more than apparent here. Moreover, the re-enactment of Boucicault's life is presented as a circus show of a kind, which is co-orchestrated by Patterson the clown. Allusions again abound, from those provided by the intertext of Boucicault's "Irish" plays such as *The Shaughraun* or the almost forgotten *The Vampire*. These are complemented by references to the story of Dr Faust (including Boucicault's own version of it) and Shakespeare's *Hamlet*. The handling of *Hamlet* is—as so much else in Parker—parodic, and concerns a ghost.

The spectre in question is the Phantom Fiddler who symbolises Boucicault's father. The Phantom Fiddler operates again at a level which is distinct from that of Boucicault's and the public's memories re-presented on the stage. As the Phantom Bride of *Northern Star*, it appears only in the first act of the two-act play. The paternal ghost is preceded by the elegiac tune of his violin, and when he enters the stage, his appearance seems quite Beckettian: "a stooped, homeless figure, shrouded in a shabby, outsize ulster. White hair hangs down from under the wide brim of his battered, dark-green hat" (87); his face is, significantly, never seen. During the *Hamlet*-like encounter with his son ("Father?" [...] "Look at me. Speak to me!" 87-88), the spectre never utters a word, and—after having witnessed a love scene involving his wife and Boucicault's foster father—simply vanishes. There seems to be a brief second apparition towards the end of the first act: this time, however, the whole intervention is merely a ghastly practical joke played by the despised clown (112-13). Needless to say, this hardly counts as exorcism; in fact, the sound of the old man's fiddle can still be heard after Patterson has performed his cruel jest (113).

The function of this ghost is again multiple. It serves to dramatise the uncertain parentage of Dion Boucicault: the playwright's nominal father, Samuel Smith Boursiquot, left his mother shortly after Dion's birth and seems to have removed himself into "the town of Athlone [...] dead in the centre of Ireland" (112). Thus, the ghost of the father attains an even deeper allegorical dimension: not only is it a voiceless, mournful spectre with an ambiguous face, but it is also a figure dwelling at the very centre of the banished country of the playwright's origin. The gloomy melancholy and fear accompanying the uncanny phantom onstage only add to the poignant dramatisation of Boucicault's uneasy relationship with the "land of his fathers." Nevertheless, the spectral father figure cannot be read in a simple nationalist key (i.e., as an allegorical embodiment of Ireland) as Boursiquot was a Huguenot wine merchant, while the rather unremarkable small town of Athlone may hardly be called the centre of Ireland in any other than a vaguely cartographic sense.

In the end, Boucicault arrives neither in Heaven nor Hell: the elaborate mechanism that elevates his catafalque with a pomp towards the firmament suddenly stops dead, and rain starts pouring through the roof (144). This suitably ironic ending does not—despite everything—leave the poor playwright in limbo: on the contrary, at the end of *Heavenly Bodies* he is firmly established in the minds of the audience. The enigmatic, bold and shameless Boucicault becomes a ghost resuscitated in his own right. In this respect, he is similar to Henry Joy McCracken of *Northern Star*, another character taken from the limbo of history by Parker and presented to the audience.

Pentecost (completed in 1987) concludes not only the trio of history plays but sadly also all of Parker's oeuvre. It is perhaps his most intensely private play, and also the one in which ghosts are finally laid to rest for good. The method chosen by Parker for this climactic piece is one of "heightened realism" (10); the form eerily corresponds to its setting in 1974 Belfast of the Ulster Worker's Council strike and to the desperate plight of its characters, all of whom are stuck in situations, private and public, from which there seems to be no escape. The crammed space and heightened ceilings of the rooms reflect the inner claustrophobia and anguish experienced by the individual characters.

The play is interspersed with biblical references, beginning with the Pentecostal symbolism reflected in the play's structure:[32] there are five characters and five scenes, culminating in a final revelation accompanied by speaking in tongues. This is combined with the presence of Christ, first in the appellation of Marian and Lenny's dead baby Christopher, but also in all "live" characters being aged thirty-three in a play that begins at Easter. Finally, the acerbic character of the returned Belfast prodigal who ends up changing his views on his hometown is appropriately called Peter, "the rock on which the Church was founded."[33]

The biblical landscape provides a backdrop to the Belfast shattered by one of the most violent moments of the sectarian conflict. Given Parker's previous depictions of the city, it is not surprising that *Pentecost* is also haunted by ghosts. Several prominent spectres pace around off-stage, each of them in the centre of the characters' life stories: the dead Christopher, Ruth's still-born children, and finally Lily's husband Alfie, her English airman lover and her abandoned illegitimate baby. However, it is the Loyalist widow Lily Matthews herself who is the only ghost to be given stage presence. Her status is really not certain though: she is invoked by the deeply depressed

32 Cf. Nicholas Kent, "A Wonderfully Brave Ending," Fairleigh, *Stewart Parker*, xi.
33 Kent, "A Wonderfully Brave Ending," xi.

Marian and may be a spectre guarding the Protestant working-class house, as much as an embodiment of Marian's thoughts initiated by her finding Lily's diary.[34]

Despite this, Lily is the ghost who is most prominently released from her predicament. Before it happens, however, the play makes clear that the haunting of Marian by Lily has become mutual: "You think you're haunting me, don't you. But you see it's me that's actually haunting you," says Marian to Lily (180) in a remark which in Richtarik's words epitomises the fact that Marian represents "the first generation of Northern Catholics, who were coming into their own in a province that had been organised for the express purpose of excluding them."[35] At the same time, it is Marian who discovers the dark secrets of Lily's past. Marian duly administers forgiveness: although she has been considering turning the house into a museum of vanished Loyalist past, after she has heard Lily speak about her trauma caused by the adulterous affair, she decides to clean up the house and live in it (202).[36] And it is in the house of the old Protestant woman with whom she realises she has so much in common that Marian in turn feels compelled to put words to her own trauma caused by the death of her baby. The final act of exorcism stresses the need for mercy and mutual understanding; this only is the way for the living to divest themselves of the dead, and for the dead to escape from the attention of the living.

General forgiveness is initiated by the epiphany that each of the four "live" characters experiences towards the end of the play. Peter, Lenny, Ruth and Marian voice and internalise these epiphanies by sharing them with the others, while the play concludes with an incantation of the passages from the *Acts of the Apostles* about the manifestation of the Holy Ghost to Christ's disciples. In a sense then, ghosts are replaced by a Ghost in *Pentecost*. However, this Ghost does not bear a strictly

---

34 Richtarik, "'Ireland, the Continuous Past,'" 272.
35 Richtarik, "'Ireland, the Continuous Past,'" 272.
36 Cf. Richtarik, "'Ireland, the Continuous Past,'" 273.

religious meaning: its message simply conveys the importance of living one's life to the full in a place like the war zone of Belfast, after coming to terms with its multiple spectres. It is a message of hope, spread by the play in a way similar to the Apostles' spreading of the Gospel.

Pentecost is undoubtedly a powerful play, although the ending may raise some questions as to its dramatic energy, being somewhat lengthy and oratorical. Yet it is also a drama in which Parker's principle of play seems to have been postponed in order to propound a strong vision of the possible foundations of a harmonious future, or in Parker's words, a "workable model of wholeness." And this is in spite of the apparent hopelessness of its characters' final situation: they are planning a future in a house which stands in the firing line and is about to be burnt down at any minute. The power of hope generated by the ritualised ending overrides any such concerns, much more strongly than in the merrily absurd ending of *Spokesong*. One way of viewing this effect is by pointing out how the play achieves control over its ironies by the force of a spiritual revelation. Transcendence is not gained by irony in *Pentecost* but by an act of spiritual purification and forgiveness which results in the reshaping of individual identity. *Pentecost* replaces the transcendence of a flawed reality of Parker's earlier work by transcendence in its original metaphysical sense, which is moreover depicted as too powerful to be treated as mere wishful thinking of those facing the horrible reality of 1974 Belfast. While it might seem paradoxical to suggest that the conflict between the Protestants and the Catholics should be resolved through what in its essence is religious belief, the play communicates this without the slightest hint of irony. Curiously enough then, Parker may be regarded as sharing some of the intellectual stages travelled by the Romantic ironist Friedrich Schlegel who also ultimately came to the conclusion that if he was to see the dawning of a Golden Age, he must return to religion.

What is also remarkable is that Parker turned in *Pentecost* for the first time towards the dominant mode of Irish drama, one couched in realism and based on the power of narrative. Given that this mode is better suited to the desire to persuasively deliver a message, the change in fact appears plausible despite Parker's unwavering commitment to joyous experimentalism, since the most important aspect of *Pentecost* seems to be precisely that it leads up to a message which is to be shared out. At the same time, Parker knew he was terminally ill when working on *Pentecost*, and the play may justifiably be regarded as the legacy of an artist who had genuinely attempted to offer in his work a potential resolution to a deeply-seated political conflict.

The Parker of *Pentecost* is perhaps no longer Lyotard's experimental artist of modernity who delights in recasting the "rules of the game." Nonetheless, this does not quite make him an author of the other category outlined by Lyotard, that is, one expressing a nostalgic desire for an unambiguous present.[37] It rather points out the hope that arises when individual people come to terms with their traumas and are able to reconfigure the narratives guiding or dominating their lives. *Pentecost* gestures firmly towards the future, without any nostalgic tendency to resuscitate an unequivocal past. Parker's sheer inventiveness and talent are summarised by Stephen Rea, who wrote in 1999: "The vacuum in Irish theatre created by the death of Stewart Parker in 1988 has expanded rather than contracted."[38]

---

[37] Lyotard, *Le postmoderne expliqué aux enfants*, 30.
[38] Stephen Rea, Introduction to Stewart Parker, *Plays: 2* (London: Methuen, 2000) ix.

"Disconcert and Destabilise the Prisoner": Martin McDonagh

Irish drama has been experiencing a gradual shift since the mid-1990s from concerns with collective identity on the one hand, and the chiefly naturalist theatrics of most canonical plays on the other. Both emergent and established playwrights have started to focus more on stories of individuals while providing as little impetus for allegorisation as possible, and at the same time have begun to explore alternative modes such as physical theatre and performance, occasionally even abolishing the traditional focus on the playwright for the sake of joint authorship or the creation of devised pieces. The background of these recent tendencies in a tradition of "authentic" collective representation has however been proving resilient and firm, and also still quite rewarding in terms of both popular and critical success.

The most remarkable case in point is provided by the work of Martin McDonagh. A dazzling star of contemporary Irish theatre, McDonagh had an incredible five plays with an Irish setting produced in rapid succession: the *Leenane Trilogy*—*The Beauty Queen of Leenane* (1996), *A Skull in Connemara* (1997) and *The Lonesome West* (1997)—and two "Aran" plays, *The Cripple of Inishmaan* (1996) and *The Lieutenant of Inishmore* (2001). All of these works are characterised by an ostentatious appropriation of the rural Ireland of Revival drama and its brutally humorous refiguration in a sitcom-cum-gangster movie vein. Part of the stunning success of McDonagh's "Irish" plays has clearly been due to their ambivalent engagement with the Irish theatrical canon, a feature that I would like to explore in what follows. At the same time, Martin McDonagh's reception by critics arguably provides remarkable insight into the recent trends in Irish theatre criticism, and further documents the resilience of the discourse of collective identity mentioned above. A closer look at the critical treatment of Martin McDonagh should serve as a fitting conclusion to a book on irony and collective identity in Irish drama.

Despite their physical and verbal violence and their subversive treatment of much of the mainstream Irish dramatic tradition, McDonagh's plays have enjoyed extreme popularity with audiences worldwide. Times have indeed changed: it is highly unlikely that any kind of theatre could trigger an equivalent of the *Playboy* riots nowadays, in Ireland or elsewhere. And those who do not like what they have heard about a particular play simply stay at home and hardly bother to object against theatre productions.

The reasons for McDonagh's popularity are multiple. First, McDonagh has managed to take full advantage of the popularity of the "Irish play," utilising its chief ingredients—a largely conservative theatrical form, vivid characters, a well-crafted plot, linguistic local colour and a setting in Ireland—as a starting point. The overall effect has been that McDonagh's plays tend to be perceived as images of Ireland of one kind or another. As the *Irish Times* critic John Waters has stated in this respect, McDonagh makes the most of the exotic nature of Ireland for spectators abroad (which is possible chiefly due to favourable preconditioning towards the easily accessible exoticism of the Emerald Isle), while at the same time exploiting "the kitschification of Ireland and its meanings in the modern world."[1] These tendencies might appear to be mutually almost exclusive. However, the validity of Waters's point is clear, as the unlikely combination allows for a multiplicity of favourable audience reactions (i.e., a wide range of spectators are bound to discover a resonance with their views of Ireland and current local stereotypes pertaining to the country).

In addition to this, McDonagh arrived on the London stage at a time when the appetite of audiences in Britain and elsewhere in Europe for the macabre and the grotesque combined with extreme violence and vulgarity had been sated by "in-yer-face theatre" (often referred to as the "cool wave"), a genre that shares a number of features with McDonagh's shenanigans.[2] This type of drama has also transposed into the theatre popular features of American independent cinema of the urban underworld, resuscitating their shock value in another medium and reviving the "coolness" of the unabashed comedy of assorted violent, foul-mouthed losers and simpletons.

The boundless intertextual creativity demonstrated by McDonagh has become rewarding ground for a number of critics who have regarded it as a clear symptom of McDonagh's postmodernism.[3] It need only be added that the multiplicity of intertextual gestures and sources of pastiche have included—as indicated above—many a famous cult movie, thereby extending the popularity of the plays from a particular kind of regular theatre-goer to a much larger group of young-ish film fans. A similar argument might be made regarding soap aficionados; indeed, as Fintan O'Toole has stated, the *Leenane Trilogy* may be

---

[1] John Waters, "The Irish Mummy: The Plays and Purpose of Martin McDonagh," *Druids, Dudes and Beauty Queens. The Changing Face of Irish Theatre*, ed. Dermot Bolger (Dublin: New Island, 2001) 48.

[2] See Aleks Sierz, *In-Yer-Face Theatre: British Drama Today* (London: Faber, 2000). Sierz has in fact devoted a section of his pioneering study of the genre to *The Beauty Queen of Leenane* (219-225).

[3] For an excellent analysis of this issue combined with a summary of earlier approaches see Clare Wallace, "'Pastiche Soup', Bad Taste, Biting Irony and Martin McDonagh," *Litteraria Pragensia* 15.29 (2005): 3-38.

viewed as "a giant soap opera, but one that makes *Twin Peaks* look like *The Riordans*."[4] A mere sketch of the playwright's involvement with other texts is revealing: *The Beauty Queen of Leenane* offers a sitcom reiteration of Tom Murphy's *Bailegangaire* and the innumerable narratives of the Irish exile. *A Skull in Connemara* literally enacts the proverbial Donnybrook Fair, while including caricatured elements of David Lynch's *Blue Velvet* (witness the policeman Tom's use of the inhaler, the general air of perversion and the encryption of truth beyond recovery). *The Lonesome West* presents an idiosyncratic version of the story of Jacob and Esau set in the atmosphere of Tracy Letts's *Killer Joe* and vaguely echoes Sam Shepard's *True West*.[5] Finally, *The Cripple of Inishmaan* proceeds to hilariously qualify the story of Flaherty's *The Man of Aran* and skilfully appropriates and reshapes elements of Synge's *Riders to the Sea*, from the old "mammy" in mourning through the constant peril of the sea down to the young Bartley's name. Virtually all the plays feature a brilliant, multifaceted exploitation of Synge's *Playboy* (noted and/or discussed by many). A rather different source of pastiche that concerns both the brutality and also the absurdity of exchanges between various characters is provided by the early works of Harold Pinter and David Mamet, as noted by Clare Wallace, who has also written on the affinity between McDonagh and another outrageous "purveyor of conscious artifice," Joe Orton.[6] Moreover, there are an infinite number of minor allusions, ranging from Friel's *Translations* (Johnnypateenmike's three items of news in *The Cripple*) to the *Father Ted* series or the early Coen brothers' films.

---

[4] Fintan O'Toole, "Murderous Laughter," *The Irish Times* 24 June 1997, reprinted in Fintan O'Toole, *Critical Moments*, eds. Julia Furay and Redmond O'Hanlon (Dublin: Carysfort Press, 2003) 180.

[5] For a detailed elaboration of the parallel see Mária Kurdi, "'Ireland mustn't be such a bad place, so, if the Yanks want to come here to do their filming.' Reflections on the West and Irishness in Martin McDonagh's Plays," *Codes and Masks: Aspects of Identity in Contemporary Irish Plays in an Intercultural Context* (Frankfurt am Main: Peter Lang, 2000) 52-54.

[6] Wallace, "'Pastiche Soup', Bad Taste, Biting Irony," 8-10.

Nonetheless, McDonagh's theatrical formula has been gradually fading, which has become apparent with *The Lieutenant of Inishmore*. Despite the fact that McDonagh spoke of the piece in his own typical manner as "his best play to date,"[7] it seemed really to be an early text written around the same time as *The Beauty Queen*,[8] which would explain the relative lack of refinement of the plot and other details when compared, for instance, with *The Cripple*. The play still abounds in rough humour, and builds on an intricate plot line; however, it is simply a fifth comedy cast virtually in the same mould. The earlier subtlety of intertextual referencing and parody has very much disappeared: *The Lieutenant* is a mere re-enactment of the blood and guts of Quentin Tarantino's *Reservoir Dogs*, combined, again, with *Killer Joe*, while throwing in a few details from *Desperado* (e.g., the brandishing of two handguns in a shootout) and *Bonnie and Clyde* for good measure (Padraic and Mairead as the romantic outlaws in Scene Eight). A potentially satirical aspect of the play perhaps resides in the critique of a stereotypical British view of the Irish as wild IRA men; but a satire based on a fairly crude and heavily dated stereotype of the Brit seems rather pointless, to say the least. All in all, the play sadly remains a rather shallow farce.

There is undeniably a sense in which *The Lieutenant* puts the audience to test: McDonagh seems to be probing at least how much blood and torture will be tolerated on the stage. But as Clare Wallace has noted, were this to be the only achievement, McDonagh's work would basically shrink to a mere presentation in the theatre of something that has long ago become the norm in contemporary cinema. In other words, all of McDonagh would rapidly turn into just another replication of the old *épater le bourgeois*.[9] Judging by the typically over-the-

---

7   Joyce Flynn, "Stage, Screen, and Another Ireland," *American Repertory Theatre News* 20 Jan. 1999.

8   Sean O'Hagan, "The Wild West," *The Guardian* 24 Mar. 2001.

9   Clare Wallace in an introduction to her paper "Versions and Reversion: Some Remarks on Contemporary Drama in Ireland," 3rd EFACIS Conference, 6-9 December 2001, University of Aarhus, Denmark.

top presentation of *The Lieutenant* by its author, this does indeed seem to be the idea: McDonagh hailed *The Lieutenant* prior to its premiere as having "more gunshots and squibs going off on stage than any play you've ever seen," while claiming about his creative effort that it was "like that great Sex Pistols' song, where [Johnny Rotten] sings "I wanna destroy passers-by." It doesn't really get any better, or simpler, than that."[10] Fortunately, it does in fact: one of the aspects *The Lieutenant* manages to retain from its predecessors is its recurrent self-reflexivity. The punk note thus receives a significant degree of qualification, ultimately in the final echo of *Waiting for Godot* which amounts to an ironic meta-reflection on the nature of the whole play, and perhaps McDonagh's entire "Irish" enterprise: "DAVEY: 'Worse and worse this story gets. […] Oh, will it never end? Will it never fecking end?' DONNY: 'It fecking won't, d'you know!'"[11]

Given the amount of talent and skill demonstrated by Martin McDonagh, expectations were running high when the production of his first non-Irish play, *The Pillowman*, was announced in 2003. Set in a fictitious totalitarian state, probably some time in the mid-twentieth century,[12] *The Pillowman* concerns a writer who has been arrested for the content of his stories. It is again a black comedy featuring graphic violence, frequent vulgarities, and moments of irresistible humour. As with McDonagh's previous plays, much of its effect is based on sudden, unexpected twists, while significant aspects of the plot are conceived basically as "a puzzle without a solution" (17). In the end, you will never know, for instance, whether Katurian's mentally handicapped brother Michal really killed the two children, an act for which he consequently ended up being murdered by Katurian.

[10] O'Hagan, "The Wild West."
[11] Martin McDonagh, *The Lieutenant of Inishmore* (London: Methuen, 2001) 64, 67.
[12] Cf. Martin McDonagh, *The Pillowman* (London: Faber, 2003) 104. Further references are given in parentheses in the text.

Moreover, McDonagh once more utilised elements of naturalist theatre within a grotesque framework in order to play with audience expectations. The opening scene, for instance, initially seems fairly realistic: a writer suffers politically motivated violence from two plain-clothes policemen. Nonetheless, the interaction grows gradually clichéd to the point of hyperbole. The linguistic mélange of names (Katurian, Tupolski, Ariel, Kamenice, etc.) only underscores the fictitious nature of the setting. On the other hand, the violence in *The Pillowman* is always presented in a gruesome, naturalist fashion which tends to regularly disrupt the hyperbolical pattern. At the same time, particular scenes seem to bring in symbolical elements and thus add to the deliberate generic instability of the play. This happens most remarkably in the re-enactment of the story of the writer and his brother which is staged in a "child's room, next door to which there is another identical room, perhaps made of glass, but padlocked and totally dark" (31), a setting symbolically suggestive of the writer's unacknowledged secrets, or perhaps his unconscious. Parallel to this, the dialogue oscillates throughout between realistic conversations, captivating storytelling, clichéd exchanges and comedy routine.

Apart from the blending of genres, *The Pillowman* is characterised by an incessant switching of themes. The initial motif of the totalitarian oppression of artists is swiftly modified as it transpires that the problem with Katurian's writing has nothing to do with politics, and the interrogation turns out to be a murder inquiry. At the same time, the weighty issue of authorial responsibility is raised: if an author writes stories which feature vivid descriptions of violence and slaughter, is he/she to blame when people interpret them as a set of instructions and proceed to commit murder? Finally perhaps, the play begins to focus on Katurian as an instance of a writer who values his work more than human life, including his own and his brother's. However, even this important concern is obscured by a series of final shifts in the plot, and ultimately by

Katurian's triumphant resurrection from the dead, an uncanny moment which indicates that the whole story of Katurian's interrogation may have been pure fiction from the start. Indeed, as one reviewer has noted, the play may appear to deal with some grave matters of ethics and authorship but it in fact backs out of any such considerations almost as soon as they emerge.[13] The reaching out towards other texts achieves another peak in *The Pillowman*, particularly as regards classical tales of the uncanny. A principal intertext in this area certainly is E.T.A. Hoffmann's famous story "The Sandman," from which the play may have derived its title.[14] Similarly to Hoffmann, McDonagh employs all his skills to make the uncanny palpable, giving control over the plot to various characters in turn and excelling in the persuasiveness of their tales and perspectives. The blurring of the borderline between reality and fiction is an essential device for both authors since, in the words of Sigmund Freud, "an uncanny effect is often and easily produced when the distinction between imagination and reality is effaced."[15] The audience of *The Pillowman* can hardly ever be sure about whether to believe what they are told—but, be it fact or fiction, they still find themselves deep in the tenets of the tale unravelling before their eyes, as the lure of the uncanny is enormous and we essentially *want* to believe in it. The play thus provides a fitting illustration of Katurian's—and McDonagh's—thesis that the writer's only duty it to tell a (terrifying) story well (7).[16]

[13] Toby Lichtig, "It Must Be the Way He Tells Them," *The Times Literary Supplement* 5252 (28 Nov. 2003): 20.

[14] For a detailed juxtaposition of the play with Hoffmann's story, see Ondřej Pilný, "Grotesque Entertainment: *The Pillowman* as Puppet Theatre," *The Theatre of Martin McDonagh: A World of Savage Stories*, eds. Lilian Chambers and Eamonn Jordan (Dublin: Carysfort Press, 2006) 217-222.

[15] Sigmund Freud, "The Uncanny," trans. James Strachey, *Pelican Freud Library* 14 (Harmondsworth: Penguin, 1985), 367.

[16] "It's definitely easier to write about things from a distance—especially when you just want to tell stories, which is all I want to do." Martin McDonagh quoted in Flynn, "Stage, Screen, and Another Ireland"; "it's always, first and

What is part and parcel of persuasive storytelling here though is shameless manipulation that takes place at multiple levels: characters are manipulated by their author, they manipulate other characters in turn while the ultimate aim is to shunt the audience to and fro in a similar way without losing a firm grip over it—or, in detective Tupolski's words, to: "Disconcert and destabilise the prisoner" (82). The characters are swung around by their creator without any apparent limit, while the flummoxed audience gradually realise they are in the same boat.[17]

I have suggested elsewhere that the aesthetic of Martin McDonagh's work may be summed up by the term grotesque entertainment,[18] and it will perhaps be useful to repeat its chief characteristics here. These include the staging of graphic, often gratuitous violence, offensive language, ubiquitous black humour and the provision of fairly crude—but hardly resistible—laughs. What is typical is the lack of depth of character psychology, and in accordance with the traditional notion of the grotesque, the mixing of disparate generic and thematic elements. Grotesque entertainment also features strategic deployment of the uncanny as a central device. Hence, inexplicable interventions from outside the presented reality abound, fictitious tales produce fatal effects, characters miraculously survive what seem to be mortal wounds or diseases in order to unexpectedly reappear, and even the dead are occasionally resurrected. Last but not least, grotesque entertainment often raises seminal questions of ethics, justice, and artistic responsibility but as a rule, all such issues are swiftly obscured by further outrageous happenings. Moral, political and artistic dilemmas then in fact seem to be introduced merely for the sake of being ultimately deemed irrelevant.

last, about story. Story is everything. Story and a bit of attitude." Martin McDonagh quoted in O'Hagan, "The Wild West."

[17] For more details see Pilný, "Grotesque Entertainment," 219.
[18] Pilný, "Grotesque Entertainment," 220-21.

It will have become apparent from my discussion so far that the aesthetic of grotesque entertainment is fundamentally formulaic, despite all the enchantment and fun it positively provides. In an early review of *The Leenane Trilogy*, Fintan O'Toole has hinted at a peculiar analogy which could be made with puppet theatre, observing that McDonagh's characters are "puppets who continue to move around long after the strings of logical control have been cut."[19] *The Pillowman* has only highlighted how apt such an analogy was, making it plain that what we are watching with McDonagh is merely a clattering puppet dance, distinctly manipulative and almost entirely dehumanised. And it is perhaps the general repetitiveness of the pattern in all the plays that is eventually disappointing.[20]

The large majority of critical reactions to McDonagh's "Irish" comedies, positive and negative alike, have however been focused in another direction. This may be explained by the fact that the overall approach in Irish drama criticism tends to be determined by the notion of Irish drama essentially holding a "mirror up to nature/nation." Indeed it is true that most of the Irish drama canon provides appropriate justification for this attitude. As Nicholas Grene asserts, canonical Irish playwrights have tended to share a sense that the country needs to be represented, and represented in an authentic manner.[21] The motivation behind this point of view has essentially been twofold. On the one hand, playwrights such as Brian Friel have found themselves circling around the political dimension of the as yet incomplete road towards national emancipation. At the same time, another impetus has been pointed out by Grene that has now become perhaps even more pervasive than ever: Irish drama is not only a distinct but also a "distinctly marketable" phenomenon.[22] When dealing with Martin McDonagh, Irish

[19] O'Toole, "Murderous Laughter," 182.
[20] I have developed the analogy at some length in an earlier article referred to above; see Pilný, "Grotesque Entertainment," 218-22.
[21] Grene, *The Politics of Irish Drama*, 2, 263.
[22] Grene, *The Politics of Irish Drama*, 262.

drama critics have then accordingly focused primarily on these issues of authenticity and/or politicality of representation, and the commercial aspect of McDonagh's enterprise.

The tendency of commentators who have seriously engaged with the plays to look for their representational features and interpret McDonagh's work around them still appears striking, however. Fintan O'Toole's generally outstanding commentaries centre around the notion of McDonagh dismantling stereotypes of Ireland, in particular the myth of the pastoral West. Nonetheless, O'Toole goes on to claim that McDonagh depicts an Ireland dislocated between the fiction of myth and the grim reality of a dysfunctional rural society. This is precisely where the implication seems to be made that the world of McDonagh's characters is to be taken as a realistic image, at least to a certain extent, one which moreover entails a certain moral judgement with regard to what is being represented.[23]

This aspect of O'Toole's perspective has been elucidated in John Waters's detailed article; it reveals the extent to which the views of O'Toole—and Waters himself—have been influenced by their own experience of growing up in rural Ireland. Waters begins by stressing that the implication that Irish audiences could or should view the exuberant spectacle presented by a McDonagh play as a realistic sketch of life in rural Ireland is an insult to their intelligence.[24] He points out, however, that it is impossible for someone who has had the real experience not to feel rather uneasy about their laughter at McDonagh's dark comedies. For the same reason, he interprets the playwright as dealing with the trauma of the material and spiritual poverty of the Irish countryside. McDonagh "deal[s] in the things which a society seeks to conceal or avoid," Waters claims, implying that what the plays really do is demonstrate the contrast between

---

[23] See for instance Fintan O'Toole, Review of *The Beauty Queen of Leenane*, *The Irish Times* 6 Feb. 1996, reprinted in O'Toole, *Critical Moments*, 159-60; "Nowhere Man," *The Irish Times* 26 Apr. 1997, or "Murderous Laughter."

[24] Waters, "The Irish Mummy," 38-39.

the very core of the foundation myth of de Valera's Republic and the actual quality of life in rural Ireland.[25]

To question the deep-felt, personal dimension of such interpretations would perhaps be beside the point. However, another perspective on McDonagh has emerged around the same time which, in contrast, is profoundly perturbing. It focuses on McDonagh's alleged complacency with the tastes of the Celtic Tiger *nouveau riche*, and seems to be driven chiefly by the anxiety that the plays of Martin McDonagh and Marina Carr may or already have become a synecdoche for Irish theatre in general. In a survey of the current state of contemporary Irish drama, Vic Merriman has attacked McDonagh for "staging Ireland as a benighted dystopia" in the framework of facile parody which also abounds in gratuitous violence "calibrated to the tastes of an aggressive bourgeois palate."[26] Merriman's argument is heavily embedded in the tradition of viewing Irish theatre as representational, while McDonagh's multiple ironies and/or any satirical dimension are deliberately ignored. Merriman essentially treats McDonagh as an author who has betrayed the cause of "genuine" Irish drama, which is to be overtly political and oppositional in a straightforward manner. Whatever attitude one adopts towards McDonagh's sky-rocketing fame and commercial success, and as much as one may legitimately be worried that McDonagh and Carr are "distorting" the picture of what was really happening in Irish theatre in the nineties, it seems alarming that Merriman needs to recall totalitarian rhetorical patterns—together with all their aesthetic intolerance and utilitarian simplifications—in order to make his point about Ireland being misrepresented again.

Despite Merriman's claims, McDonagh has been repeatedly viewed as satirising or caricaturing the myths and stereotypes of Ireland and the Irish. Yet as far as satire of contemporary Irish society is concerned, Werner Huber has quite aptly noted

[25] Waters, "The Irish Mummy," 53 and passim.
[26] Vic Merriman, "Settling for More: Excess and Success in Contemporary Irish Drama," *Druids, Dudes and Beauty Queens*, 59.

that: "The value system of the McDonagh universe appears in constant flux and in a state of destabilization" and the world of the characters is overwhelmed by constant "codding" which completely obliterates the truth about past events. This means that straightforward social satire inevitably "loses sight of its targets."[27] Nonetheless, there is another sense in which McDonagh clearly operates as a satirist: his plays in fact ironise the very notion of Irish dramatic realism. Replicating its traditionalist theatrics and utilising a distinctively constructed Hiberno-English dialect, McDonagh instigates in his audiences particular genre expectations. These he proceeds to thoroughly subvert by his gallows humour, vulgarity, historically improbable references (for instance, his 1934 Inishmaan features Johnnypateenmike making beetroot paella, Auntie Kate speaking of driving cars and the local shop selling fancy confectionery)[28] and a propensity to endow his characters with a variety of outrageous moral deficiencies which are often accompanied by a certain lack of mental capacity.

McDonagh's plays at the same time progressively satirise the pervasive concern of Irish theatre discourse with the issue of Irish identity, simply by painting an absurd, degenerated picture of "what the Irish are like." The tendency is at its strongest in *The Cripple of Inishmaan*, a play which explicitly engages with the issue of representation by letting the audience watch a grotesque onstage audience watch an image of themselves (Robert Flaherty's pseudo-documentary *The Man of Aran*, viewed by the locals as "A pile of fecking shite")[29] and by its constant mirthful variation of the claim that "Ireland mustn't be such a bad place so" if all the Americans, Germans, French, dentists, etc. want to come there to benefit and enjoy, while the

[27] Werner Huber, "The Plays of Martin McDonagh," *Twentieth-Century Theatre and Drama in English. Festschrift for Heinz Kosok on the Occasion of his 65th Birthday*, ed. Jürgen Kamm (Trier: Wissenschaftlicher Verlag Trier, 1999) 568.

[28] Martin McDonagh, *The Cripple of Inishmaan* (London: Methuen, 1997) 10-11, 36, 39, 46, 58.

[29] McDonagh, *The Cripple*, 61.

actual audience are being overwhelmed by the opportunism, lies and violence of the "Irish" onstage.

Another quite telling feature is McDonagh's focus on the general tendency of Irish nationalism to constantly refer back to an inequitable history which is seen as the chief constitutive element and legitimising force of Irishness. McDonagh's plays repeatedly mock the incapability of individual characters to be reconciled with elements of the past. Beginning with the absurd grudges over a confiscated tennis ball in *The Beauty Queen of Leenane*, through similar rancour over boys urinating in the churchyard in *A Skull in Connemara*, the vendetta threatening several characters in *The Lieutenant of Inishmore* after the death of the cat has been discovered, and Mammy's failure in *The Cripple* to come to terms with the death of her husband which occurred sixty years previously, the chain of motifs culminates on a more serious note in *The Lonesome West* with the attempt of the central characters Coleman and Valene to forget about all their mutual grievances, while their whole relationship has in fact revolved around hatred and spite. The inability to move on from past concerns, to "let bygones be bygones"[30] thus makes for an additional provocative comment within the framework of McDonagh's commentary on the discourse of collective identity.

This brand of satire constitutes a specific mimetic dimension of McDonagh which is, needless to say, distinctly different from any realistic mirroring: McDonagh's plays ironically reflect constitutive themes of Irish culture and satirically explore the expectations of particular audiences. It may be added that such ironic reflexivity forms yet another—and, from a certain perspective, the most important—link between McDonagh's work and Synge's *Playboy*, as the *Playboy* satirised in a similar way the concerns of its urban nationalist audiences and creatively manipulated their expectations, rather than having mirrored life in the West of Ireland. Synge's claim that if Ireland considers itself a healthy, living country, people should not

---

[30] Martin McDonagh, *A Skull in Connemara* (London: Methuen, 1997) 5.

"mind being laughed at without malice, as the people in every country have been laughed at in their comedies"[31] also apparently continues to resonate.

It has proved expedient when examining the schematic nature of McDonagh's aesthetic to turn towards the Romantic master of paradox, Heinrich von Kleist and his essay "On the Marionette Theatre,"[32] and extend the analogy between Martin McDonagh and a puppet master.[33] The same ironic essay, however, proceeds from discussing the mechanical but apparently graceful nature of the puppet dance to considering another central image, which in its turn bears relevance to the dominant brand of Irish writing and criticism centred on the essentialist notion of authentic representation, particularly that of collective identity. Kleist's narrator tells the story of a youngster who has lost his original grace and innocence by imitating a masterful statue of a boy extracting a splinter from his foot. After the narrator has laughingly pointed out the young man's vanity, the repetition takes on an endless quality, ensnaring the young man forever in front of a mirror in a vain attempt at the same gesture. "An invisible and incomprehensible power seemed to settle like a steel net over the free play of his gestures," observes the astonished narrator.[34] The above remarks on the position of Martin McDonagh's work within the critical discourse of Irishness have aimed to show that McDonagh has played a role similar to the narrator in Kleist's parable. His plays have pointed out the essential narcissism of writing and criticism that has continued to insist on the need to reproduce over and over again an image of a graceful nation that has been injured, be it called post-

31 J.M. Synge, Preface to *The Tinker's Wedding*, *Collected Works*, IV.3.
32 Heinrich von Kleist, "Über das Marionettentheater" (1810), *Werke und Briefe in vier Bänden, Bd. 3—Philosophische und ästetische Schriften*, hrsg. Siegfried Streller (Berlin: Aufbau Verlag, 1993) 473-480.
33 See Pilný, "Grotesque Entertainment," 219-22.
34 Heinrich von Kleist, "On the Marionette Theatre," trans. Idris Parry, *Heinrich von Kleist, Charles Baudelaire, Rainer Maria Rilke, Essays on Dolls* (London: Syrens, 1994) 9.

Greene, David H. "J.M. Synge: A Reappraisal." *Critical Essays on John Millington Synge*. Ed. Daniel J. Casey. New York: G.K. Hall/ Toronto: Maxwell Macmillan Canada, 1994. 15-27.

——, and Edward M. Stephens, *J.M. Synge, 1871-1909*. New York: Collier Books, 1961.

Gregory, Lady Augusta. *Our Irish Theatre: A Chapter of Autobiography*. New York: Oxford University Press/ Gerrards Cross: Colin Smythe, 1972.

——. *Seventy Years: Being the Autobiography of Lady Gregory*. Ed. Colin Smythe. Gerrards Cross: Colin Smythe, 1973.

Grene, Nicholas. "Approaches to The Playboy." *John Millington Synge's The Playboy of the Western World*. Ed. Harold Bloom. New York: Chelsea House, 1988. 75-88.

——. "Friel and Transparency." *Irish University Review* 29.1 (1999): 136-44.

——. *Synge: A Critical Study of the Plays*. London and Basingstoke: Macmillan, 1975.

——. "Synge's *The Shadow of the Glen*: Repetition and Allusion." *Critical Essays on John Millington Synge*. Ed. Daniel J. Casey. New York: G.K. Hall/ Toronto: Maxwell Macmillan Canada, 1994. 81-86.

——. *The Politics of Irish Drama. Plays in Context from Boucicault to Friel*. Cambridge: Cambridge University Press, 1999.

Guinness, Selina. "The Year of the Undead." *New Voices in Irish Criticism*. Ed. P.J. Mathews. Dublin and Portland: Four Courts Press, 2000. 19-27.

Henry, P.L. "The Playboy of the Western World." *Philologica Pragensia* 3 (1965): 189-204.

Hoffmann, E.T.A. "The Sandman." *Tales of Hoffmann*. Trans. R.J. Hollingdale. Harmondsworth: Penguin, 1982. 85-125.

Hogan, Robert, and James Kilroy. *The Abbey Theatre: The Years of Synge 1905-1909*. Dublin: The Dolmen Press, 1978.

Howes, Marjorie. *Yeats's Nations. Gender, Class, and Irishness*. Cambridge: Cambridge University Press, 1996.

Huber, Werner. "The Plays of Martin McDonagh." *Twentieth-Century Theatre and Drama in English. Festschrift for Heinz Kosok on the Occasion of his 65th Birthday*. Ed. Jürgen Kamm. Trier: Wissenschaftlicher Verlag Trier, 1999. 555-71.

Hunt, Hugh. *The Abbey – Ireland's National Theatre 1904-1978*. Dublin: Gill and Macmillan, 1979.

Hutcheon, Linda. *Irony's Edge. The Theory and Politics of Irony*. London and New York: Routledge, 1994.

Hyde, Douglas. *Selected Plays*. Eds. Gareth W. Dunleavy and Janet Egleson Dunleavy. Gerrards Cross: Colin Smythe, 1991.

Isidor ze Sevilly. *Etymologiae I-III*. Latin-Czech edition. Trans. Daniel Korte. Praha: Oikoymenh, 2000.

Jeffares, A. Norman. *W.B. Yeats*. London: Hutchinson, 1988.

——, and A.S. Knowland, *A Commentary on the Collected Plays of W.B. Yeats*. London: Macmillan, 1975.

Johnston, Denis. "O'Casey in the Twenties." *The O'Casey Enigma*. Ed. Micheál Ó hAodha. Cork and Dublin: Mercier Press, 1980. 20-33.

——. *Orders and Desecrations: The Life of the Playwright Denis Johnston*. Ed. Rory Johnston. Dublin: Lilliput Press, 1992.

——. *The Old Lady Says "No!"* Ed. Christine St. Peter. Washington, D.C.: The Catholic University of America Press/ Gerrards Cross: Colin Smythe, 1992.

——. "Sean O'Casey: An Appreciation." *Daily Telegraph* 11 Mar. 1926. Reprinted in *Sean O'Casey: Modern Judgments*. Ed. Ronald Ayling. London: Macmillan, 1969. 82-85.

——. *Selected Plays of Denis Johnston*. Ed. Joseph Ronsley. Gerrards Cross: Colin Smythe, 1983.

Joyce, James. *Exiles. The Essential James Joyce*. Ed. Harry Levin. London: Grafton Books, 1977. 367-436.

——. *Finnegans Wake*. Harmondsworth: Penguin, 1992.

——. *Ulysses*. Harmondsworth: Penguin, 1992.

Kearney, Richard. "Language Play: Brian Friel and Ireland's Verbal Theatre." *Studies* 62 (1983): 20-56.

——. "Myth and Motherland." Field Day Theatre Company, *Ireland's Field Day*. London: Hutchinson, 1985. 59-80.

Kennelly, Brendan, ed. *Landmarks of Irish Drama*. London: Methuen, 1988.

Kenner, Hugh. "The Living World of the Text: The Playboy." *John Millington Synge's The Playboy of the Western World*. Ed. Harold Bloom. New York: Chelsea House, 1988. 117-29.

Kiberd, Declan. *Inventing Ireland. The Literature of the Modern Nation*. London: Vintage, 1996.

——. *Synge and the Irish Language*. 2nd ed. Dublin: Gill and Macmillan, 1993.

Kierkegaard, Søren. *The Concept of Irony with Continual Reference to Socrates*. Eds. and trans. Howard V. Hong and Edna H. Hong. Princeton: Princeton University Press, 1989.

Kilroy, James F. "The Playboy as Poet." *Critical Essays on John Millington Synge*. Ed. Daniel J. Casey. New York: G.K. Hall/ Toronto: Maxwell Macmillan Canada, 1994. 119-25.

——. *The 'Playboy Riots.'* Dublin: Dolmen Press, 1971.

Kirkland, Richard. *Literature and Culture in Northern Ireland since 1965: Moments of Danger*. London and New York: Addison Wesley Longman, 1996.

von Kleist, Heinrich. "On the Marionette Theatre." Trans. Idris Parry. *Heinrich von Kleist, Charles Baudelaire, Rainer Maria Rilke, Essays on Dolls*. London: Syrens, 1994. 1-12.

——. "Über das Marionettentheater" [1810]. *Werke und Briefe in vier Bänden, Bd. 3 – Philosophische und ästetische Schriften*. Hrsg. Siegfried Streller. Berlin: Aufbau Verlag, 1993. 473-480.

Knowlson, James. *Damned to Fame. The Life of Samuel Beckett*. London: Bloomsbury Publishing, 1996.

——, and John Pilling. *Frescoes of the Skull. The Late Prose and Drama of Samuel Beckett*. London: Calder, 1979.

Knox, Dilwyn. *Ironia: Medieval and Renaissance Ideas on Irony*. Leiden: E.J. Brill, 1989.

Kosok, Heinz. "Two Irish Perspectives on World War I: Bernard Shaw and Sean O'Casey." *Hungarian Journal of English and American Studies* 2.2 (1996): 17-29.

Kurdi, Mária. *Codes and Masks: Aspects of Identity in Contemporary Irish Plays in an Intercultural Context*. Frankfurt am Main: Peter Lang, 2000.

Lang, Candance D. *Irony/Humor (Critical Paradigms)*. Baltimore and London: The Johns Hopkins University Press, 1988.

Laurence, Dan H., and Nicholas Grene, eds. *Shaw, Lady Gregory and the Abbey. A Correspondence an a Record*. Gerrards Cross: Colin Smythe, 1993.

Leblanc, Gérard. "Ironic Reversal as Theme and Technique in Synge's Shorter Comedies." *Aspects of the Irish Theatre*. Eds. Patrick Rafroidi, Raymonde Popet and William Parker. Paris: Editions Universitaires, 1972. 51-63.

Lichtig, Toby. "It Must Be the Way He Tells Them." *The Times Literary Supplement* 5252 (28 Nov. 2003): 20.

Longley, Edna. *From Cathleen to Anorexia*. Dublin: The Attic Press, 1990.

Lyotard, Jean-François. *La condition postmoderne*. Paris: Editions de Minuit, 1979.

——. *Le postmoderne expliqué aux enfants*. Paris: Editions Galilée, 1986.

——. *The Postmodern Explained to Children*. Trans. Julian Pefanis, Morgan Thomas, et al. London: Turnaround, 1992.

de Man, Paul. "Allegory and Irony in Baudelaire." *Romanticism and Contemporary Criticism*. Eds. E.S. Burt, Kevin Newmark and Andrzej Warminski. Baltimore: The Johns Hopkins University Press, 1993. 101-19.

——. "The Concept of Irony." *Aesthetic Ideology*. Ed. Andrzej Warminski. Minneapolis and London: University of Minnesota Press, 1996. 163-84.

Matthews, P.J. *Revival. The Abbey Theatre, Sinn Féin, The Gaelic League and the Co-operative Movement*. Cork: Cork University Press/ Field Day, 2003.

Maxwell, D.E.S. *A Critical History of Modern Irish Drama 1891-1980*. Cambridge: Cambridge University Press, 1984.

——. "Waiting for Emmet." *Denis Johnston: A Retrospective*. Ed. Joseph Ronsley. Gerrards Cross: Colin Smythe, 1981. 24-37.

Mc Cormack, W.J. *Fool of the Family. A Life of J.M. Synge*. New York: New York University Press, 2000.

——. *From Burke to Beckett. Ascendancy, Tradition and Betrayal in Literary History*. Cork: Cork University Press, 1994.

McDonagh, Martin. *The Beauty Queen of Leenane*. London: Methuen, 1996.

——. *The Cripple of Inishmaan*. London: Methuen, 1997.

——. *The Lieutenant of Inishmore*. London: Methuen, 2001.

——. *The Lonesome West*. London: Methuen, 1997.

——. *The Pillowman*. London: Faber, 2003.

——. *A Skull in Connemara*. London: Methuen, 1997.

McGuinness, Frank. *Plays 1*. London: Faber, 1996.

Merriman, Vic. "Settling for More: Excess and Success in Contemporary Irish Drama." *Druids, Dudes and Beauty Queens. The Changing Face of Irish Theatre*. Ed. Dermot Bolger. Dublin: New Island, 2001. 55-71.

Muecke, D.C. *The Compass of Irony*. London and New York: Methuen, 1969; 2nd ed. 1980.

——. *Irony and the Ironic*. London and New York: Methuen, 1970; 2nd ed. 1982.

Murphy, Tom. *After Tragedy: Three Irish Plays*. London: Methuen, 1988.

Murray, Christopher, ed. *Brian Friel. Essays, Diaries, Interviews: 1964-1999*. London and New York: Faber, 1999.

——. A review of *Translations*. *Irish University Review* 11.2 (1981): 238-39.

——. *Seán O'Casey: Writer at Work*. Dublin: Gill and Macmillan, 2004.

——. *Twentieth-Century Irish Drama. Mirror up to Nation*. Manchester: Manchester University Press, 1997.

O'Brien, Flann (Myles na gCopaleen). *The Poor Mouth*. Trans. Patrick C. Power. London: Hart Davis, MacGibbon, 1973.

O'Casey, Sean. *Cock-a-doodle Dandy*. Ed. David Krause. Washington, D.C.: The Catholic University of America Press/ Gerrards Cross: Colin Smythe, 1991.

——. *Rose and Crown*. New York: Macmillan, 1956.

——. *Three Plays*. London: Macmillan/ New York: St Martin's Press, 1968.

——. *Three More Plays*. London: Macmillan/ New York: St Martin's Press, 1969.

O'Hagan, Sean. "The Wild West." *The Guardian* 24 Mar. 2001.

O'Toole, Fintan. *Critical Moments*. Eds. Julia Furay and Redmond O'Hanlon. Dublin: Carysfort Press, 2003.

——. "Nowhere Man." *The Irish Times* 26 Apr. 1997.

——. "The Man from God Knows Where: Interview with Brian Friel." *In Dublin* 165 (1982): 20-27.

Parker, Stewart. *Dramatis Personae*. John Malone Memorial Lecture. Belfast: Queen's University, 1986.

——. *Plays: 1*. London: Methuen, 2000.

——. *Plays: 2*. London: Methuen, 2000.

——. "State of Play." *The Canadian Journal of Irish Studies* 7.1 (June 1981): 5-11.

——. *Three Plays for Ireland*. London: Oberon Books, 1989.

Parry, Alan, and Robert E. Doan. *Story Re-Visions: Narrative Therapy in the Post-Modern World*. New York: The Guilford Press, 1994.

Paulin, Tom. "Riders to the Sea: A Revisionist Tragedy?" *Interpreting Synge: Essays from the Synge Summer School, 1991-2000*. Ed. Nicholas Grene. Dublin: Lilliput Press, 2000. 111-116.

Pearse, Padraic H. *Collected Works of Pádraic H. Pearse: Political Writings and Speeches*. Dublin: Phoenix, 1924.

——. *O'Donovan Rossa's Funeral. Address at Graveside by P.H. Pearse*. Dublin: The Office of Public Works, n.d.

Pethica, James. "'A Young Man's Ghost': Lady Gregory and J.M. Synge." *Irish University Review* 34.1 (2004): 1-20.

Pilkington, Lionel. "'Every Crossing Sweeper Thinks Himself a Moralist': The Critical Role of Audiences in Irish Theatre History." *Irish University Review* 27.1 (1997): 152-65.

——. *Theatre and the State in Twentieth-Century Ireland. Cultivating the People*. London and New York: Routledge, 2001.

Pilný, Ondřej. "Concepts of Irony." *Acta Universitatis Carolinae – Philologica* 2 (2005)/ Prague Studies in English XXIV. Prague: The Karolinum Press, 2006. 141-56.

——. "Grotesque Entertainment: *The Pillowman* as Puppet Theatre." *The Theatre of Martin McDonagh: A World of Savage Stories*. Eds. Lilian Chambers and Eamonn Jordan. Dublin: Carysfort Press, 2006. 214-223.

Price, Alan. "The Dramatic Imagination: The Playboy" *John Millington Synge's The Playboy of the Western World*. Ed. Harold Bloom. New York: Chelsea House, 1988. 19-37.

Procházka, Martin. "Seasons in K.H. Mácha's *May* and Byron's Poetry: A Reading of Two Ironical Strategies." *Byron: A Poet for All Seasons*. Ed. Marios Byron Raizis. Messolonghi: Messolonghi Byron Society, 2000. 209-19.

Puttenham, George. *The Arte of English Poesie* [1589]. Ed. Edward Arber. London: n.p., 1896.

Quilligan, Patrick. "Field Day's New Double Bill." *The Irish Times* 18 Sept. 1984: 10.

Quintilianus. *Základy rétoriky* [Institutionis oratoriae libri XII]. Trans. V. Bahník. Praha: Odeon, 1985.

Richards, Shaun. "Field Day's Fifth Province: Avenue or Impasse?" *Culture and Politics in Northern Ireland, 1960-1990*. Ed. Eamonn Hughes. Buckingham and Bristol, PA: Open University Press, 1991. 139-49.

Richtarik, Marilynn J. *Acting between the Lines: The Field Day Theatre Company and Irish Cultural Politics 1980-1984*. Oxford: Clarendon Press, 1994.

——. "'Ireland, the Continuous Past': Stewart Parker's Belfast History Plays." *A Century of Irish Drama: Widening the Stage*. Eds. Stephen

Watt, Eileen Morgan and Shakir Mustafa. Bloomington and Indianapolis: Indiana University Press, 2000. 256-74.

Roche, Anthony. "The Two Worlds of Synge's The Well of the Saints." *Critical Essays on John Millington Synge*. Ed. Daniel J. Casey. New York: G.K. Hall/ Toronto: Maxwell Macmillan Canada, 1994. 98-107.

Rorty, Richard. *Contingency, Irony and Solidarity*. Cambridge: Cambridge University Press, 1989.

Royle, Nicholas. *The Uncanny*. Manchester: Manchester University Press, 2003.

Saddlemyer, Ann, ed. *The Collected Letters of John Millington Synge I*. Oxford: Clarendon Press, 1983.

——. *Theatre Business. The Correspondence of the First Abbey Theatre Directors*. University Park and London: The Pennsylvania State University Press, 1982.

Satake, Akiko. "The Seven Ages of Harry Joy McCracken: Stewart Parker's Northern Star as a History Play of the United Irishmen in 1798." *Theatre Stuff: Critical Essays on Contemporary Irish Theatre*. Ed. Eamonn Jordan. Dublin: Carysfort Press, 2000. 176-86.

Schlegel, Friedrich. *Charakteristiken und Kritiken I (1796-1801)*. Hrsg. Hans Eichner. München: Verlag Ferd. Schöningh/ Zürich: Thomas Verlag, 1967.

Schnell, Ralf. *Die verkehrte Welt. Literarische Ironie im 19. Jahrhundert*. Stuttgart: J.B. Metzlersche Verlagsbuchhandlung, 1989.

Shaw, G.B. *The Complete Plays of Bernard Shaw*. London: Hamlyn, 1965.

Sierz, Aleks. *In-Yer-Face Theatre: British Drama Today*. London: Faber, 2000.

Spacks, Patricia Meyer. "The Making of The Playboy." *John Millington Synge's The Playboy of the Western World*. Ed. Harold Bloom. New York: Chelsea House, 1988. 7-17.

Steiner, George. *After Babel*. London: Oxford University Press, 1977.

Stork, Uwe. *Der sprachliche Rhythmus in den Bühnenstücken John Millington Synges*. Inaugural dissertation. Freiburg i. Br.: n.p., 1969.

Synge, John Millington. *Collected Works I: Poems*. Ed. Robin Skelton. Oxford: Oxford University Press, 1962; Gerrards Cross: Colin Smythe/ Washington: The Catholic University of America Press, 1982.

——. *Collected Works II: Prose*. Ed. Alan Price. Oxford: Oxford University Press, 1966; Gerrards Cross: Colin Smythe/ Washington: The Catholic University of America Press, 1982.

——. *Collected Works III: Plays, Book 1*. Ed. Ann Saddlemyer. Oxford: Oxford University Press, 1968; Gerrards Cross: Colin Smythe/ Washington: The Catholic University of America Press, 1982.

——. *Collected Works IV: Plays, Book 2*. Ed. Ann Saddlemyer. Oxford: Oxford University Press, 1968; Gerrards Cross: Colin Smythe/ Washington: The Catholic University of America Press, 1982.

——. *Plays, Poems and Prose*. Ed. Alison Smith. London: J.M. Dent/ Rutland, Vermont: Charles Tuttle, 1992.

——. *Hrdina západu*. Trans. Martin Hilský. Praha: Národní divadlo, 1996.

Vickers, Brian. *In Defence of Rhetoric*. Oxford: Clarendon Press, 1998.

Vico, Giambattista. *Základy nové vědy o společné přirozenosti národů* [Principi di scienza nuova d'intorno alla comune natura delle nazioni]. Trans. Martin Quotidian. Praha: Academia, 1991.

Wallace, Clare. "'Pastiche Soup', Bad Taste, Biting Irony and Martin McDonagh." *Litteraria Pragensia* 15.29 (2005): 3-38.

Waters, John. "The Irish Mummy: The Plays and Purpose of Martin McDonagh." *Druids, Dudes and Beauty Queens. The Changing Face of Irish Theatre*. Ed. Dermot Bolger. Dublin: New Island, 2001. 30-54.

Watzlawick, Paul, Janet Beavin Bavelas, and Don D. Jackson. *Pragmatics of Human Communication: A Study of Interactional Patterns, Pathologies, and Paradoxes*. New York and London: Norton, 1967.

——. *Menschliche Kommunikation: Formen, Störungen, Paradoxien*. Bern und Stuttgart: Verlag Hans Huber, 1969.

White, Hayden. *Metahistory. The Historical Imagination in Nineteenth-Century Europe*. Baltimore and London: The Johns Hopkins University Press, 1973.

——. *Tropics of Discourse. Essays in Cultural Criticism*. Baltimore: The Johns Hopkins University Press, 1978.

Wordsworth, William, and Samuel Taylor Coleridge. *Lyrical Ballads 1798*. Ed. W.J.B. Owen. London: Oxford University Press, 1967.

Worth, Katherine. *The Irish Drama of Europe from Yeats to Beckett*. London: The Athlone Press, 1978.

Yeats, William Butler. *Collected Poems*. Ed. Augustine Martin. London: Vintage, 1992.

——. *Collected Works II: The Plays*. Ed. David R. Clark and Rosalind E. Clark. Houndmills and New York: Palgrave, 2001.

——. *Explorations*. New York: Macmillan, 1962.

——. "Preface to the First Edition of The Well of the Saints." John Millington Synge, *Collected Works III: Plays Book 1*. Ed. Ann Saddlemyer. Oxford: Oxford University Press, 1968; Gerrards Cross: Colin Smythe/ Washington: The Catholic University of America Press, 1982. 63-68.

——, ed. *The Oxford Book of Modern Verse 1892-1935*. Oxford: Clarendon Press, 1936.

Index

Abbey Theatre, 1, 5, 14, 16, 19, 20, 30, 35, 43-4, 52, 54, 62-3, 65, 71-5, 80-1, 83, 85-6, 101-2, 135
AE (George Russell), 27, 33
agit-prop, 77, 136
allegory, 28, 31, 33, 46, 78, 86, 95-7, 115, 145, 149, 154
Allgood, Molly, 37
Andrews, Elmer, 138
Aran Islands, 37-9, 42-4, 48, 53, 154
Aristotle, 81
Arnold, Matthew, 16
Ascendancy, 15-7, 25, 28
Austin, J.L., 100
authenticity, 4, 38, 41, 154, 163, 168
Bagenal, Mabel, 108
Barthes, Roland, 109
Beckett, Samuel, 7, 39, 56, 143, 144, 148; *Waiting for Godot*, 56, 159
Behan, Brendan, 144
Bigley, Bruce M., 60, 63
Blake, William, 99-100
Bonnie and Clyde, 158
Booth, Wayne C., 3
Boucicault, Dion, 147-9; *The Shaughraun*, 148
Boyle, William, 65-6; *The Building Fund*, 66
Brecht, Bertolt, 137, 143

British Army, 81, 115
Brooks, Cleanth, 49
Canfield, Curtis, 87, 88, 91, 94
Čapek, Josef, 87; *The Land of Many Names*, 87
Carr, Marina, 7, 165
Carthage, 117-8
Celtic Tiger, 6, 165
Celticism, 13, 16-17
Civil War, 75
Clarke, Austin, 75
Coen brothers, 157
Coleridge, Samuel Taylor, 19-20
collage, 87, 98, 101, 147
Colum, Padraic, 63
communication, 3, 5, 107, 120-8, 130-1, 133
Connelly, Marc, 87; *Beggar on Horseback*, 87
Connolly, Sean, 108, 114
Craig, Gordon, 31
Cúchulainn, 15, 43, 59
Cumann na nGaedheal, 77
Curran, Sarah, 92, 95, 99
dance, 6, 79, 90, 99, 128-31, 139, 141, 147, 163, 168
Dantanus, Ulf, 109, 116-7
de Man, Paul, 3
de Valera, Éamon, 165

Dean, Joan FitzPatrick, 27-8, 30, 48, 52, 75, 102

Deane, Seamus, 105-7, 109-14, 119-20

deconstruction, 91, 139-40

Derrida, Jacques, 100, 139-40

double bind, 123

Drama League, 73, 86

Duggan, G.C., 13

Easter Rising, 75

Eglinton, John, 27

Emmet, Robert, 87-8, 91-5, 98-100

experimentalism, 1, 6, 13-4, 24, 72, 81, 101-2, 135, 137, 146, 153, 169

expressionism, 78, 87-8, 97, 101-2

Famine, 29

farce, 54, 57, 61, 78, 127, 142, 158

Farquhar, George, 144

Father Ted, 157

Fay, Frank, 32-3

Fay, W.G., 32-3, 47

Ferrar, Harold, 85, 94, 101

Field Day, 2, 5, 8, 105-14, 119, 121, 123, 127, 131-3, 136

Fifth Province, 131-2

Flannery, James W., 14, 17-9, 31, 39, 74

folklore, 15, 48

Foster, R.F., 12, 14-7, 19, 24-5, 27, 29-30, 33, 36, 73-5, 78, 80-1, 83, 102

Foucault, Michel, 57-8

Frazier, Adrian, 16, 18, 21, 23-30, 32-4, 36, 42, 45, 47, 49, 62

Free State, 77, 85, 93

Freud, Sigmund, 161

Friel, Brian, 3, 5, 6, 8, 76, 105, 107-9, 113-21, 123-8, 131, 133, 157, 163; *The Communication Cord*, 119, 126-7; *Dancing at Lughnasa*, 127-31; *Faith Healer*, 120, 123-5; *The Freedom of the City*, 108; *Making History*, 108-9, 119; *Philadelphia, Here I Come*, 121;

Translations, 108-9, 113-8, 125-6, 157

Furst, Lilian R., 3, 139

Gaelic League, 13, 19, 21, 102

gangster movie, 6, 154

Gate Theatre, 73

ghosts and spectres, 6-7, 46, 89, 137, 140-51

Golden Age, 14, 139, 152

Gonne, Maud, 21, 31, 36

Grattan, Henry, 93, 96

Greek theatre, 14, 58

Gregory, lady Augusta, 1, 11-3, 15-7, 20-2, 24-6, 30-1, 33-4, 36, 43, 45, 62-3, 73, 80, 85, 86, 91, 95, 116; *Spreading the News*, 20

Grene, Nicholas, 38-9, 45, 49, 51, 60-1, 63, 73, 76, 81-2, 86, 88-9, 94, 102, 123-4, 131, 147, 163

Griffith, Arthur, 36, 48

grotesque, 6, 57, 90, 156, 160, 162-3, 166

Gwynn, Stephen, 31-2

Hammond, David, 105

Heaney, Seamus, 105

Henry, P.L., 40

Herder, Johann Gottfried von, 19

heroism, 5, 14, 37, 44, 57, 59, 75, 78-9, 87, 91-2, 94, 95, 100-1

Hilský, Martin, 40

Hoffmann, E.T.A., 161

Hogan, Robert, 62-3, 65

Horniman, Annie, 16, 24, 72

Howes, Marjorie, 16, 23, 25, 28, 35

Huber, Werner, 122, 165, 166

Huizinga, Johan, 137

Hunt, Hugh, 43, 83

Hutcheon, Linda, 3

Hyde, Douglas, 39, 50

hyperbole, 6, 143, 160

Ibsen, Henrik, 14, 21, 49, 73

intertextuality, 3, 85-6, 90, 97, 99, 148, 156, 158, 161

Invincibles, 99

Irish Literary Theatre, 1, 11-4, 16-8, 23-5, 27, 30, 32, 42, 49, 102

irony, 2-7, 11-2, 34-5, 41-2, 45-6, 49-54, 56, 58-61, 64, 66-7, 71, 76, 78, 80, 94, 100-2, 116, 119, 125, 131, 136-40, 144, 148-9, 152, 155, 159, 165-8

Johnston, Denis, 2, 5, 33, 71, 75, 77, 85-91, 93-5, 98-101, 146; *The Moon in the Yellow River*, 101; *The Old Lady Says "No!"* 5, 71, 85-102

Joyce, James, 28, 33, 72, 74, 81, 88-9, 158; *Exiles*, 72, 74, 81; *Finnegans Wake*, 89; *Ulysses*, 88, 90

Kaiser, Georg, 87

Kaufman, George S., 87

Kearney, Richard, 109, 111, 113, 117

Kenner, Hugh, 40, 61

Kettle, Tom, 34

Khayyam, Omar, 100

Kiberd, Declan, 16, 38-9, 44, 52, 59-60, 64, 66, 74, 76-7, 79, 81, 82

Kilroy, James, 62-3, 65

Kilroy, Thomas, 105

Kilwarden, Lord Chief Justice, 100

Kirkland, Richard, 112

Kleist, Heinrich von, 168

Knowlson, James, 56

Kosok, Heinz, 80-1, 166

Kurdi, Mária, 157

Laurence, Dan H., 73

Lebeau, Henri, 52

Leblanc, Gérard, 50-1

Lecky, William Edward Hartpole, 32

Letts, Tracy, 157; *Killer Joe*, 157-8

Lévi-Strauss, Claude, 129

Longley, Edna, 111, 132-3

Lynch, David, 157

Lyotard, Jean-François, 5, 106-7, 131, 133, 137-8, 153

MacKenna, Stephen, 43

Macleod, Fiona, 16

MacNamara, Brinsley, 75, 102

Mamet, David, 157

Markievicz, Constance, 32

Martyn, Edward, 12

Mathews, P.J., 19, 33

Maxwell, D.E.S., 42, 87-8, 99

Mc Cormack, W.J., 15-6

McCracken, Henry Joy, 144-7, 149

McDonagh, Martin, 2, 6, 8, 154-68; *The Beauty Queen of Leenane*, 154, 156-8, 164, 167; *The Cripple of Inishmaan*, 154, 157-8, 166-7; *Leenane Trilogy*, 154, 156, 163; *The Lieutenant of Inishmore*, 154, 158-9, 167; *The Lonesome West*, 154, 157, 167; *The Pillowman*, 159-61, 163; *A Skull in Connemara*, 154, 157, 167

McGuinness, Frank, 118, 132; *Carthaginians*, 118; *Observe the Sons of Ulster*, 132

McMullan, Anna, 131

Merriman, Vic, 165

metanarrative, 2, 4-5, 11, 27, 105-6, 110-14, 119-20, 131

micro-narrative, 5, 107, 110-1, 113-4, 120, 131, 133

Milne, A.A., 93

mimesis, 23, 64, 140, 142, 144, 167

modernism, 5, 67, 74, 86, 102

Molière, 60

Moran, D.P., 21

Morgan, Charles, 83

Muecke, D.C., 2, 3

Murphy, Tom, 6, 157; *Bailegangaire*, 157

Murphy, W.M., 21

Murray, Christopher, 42, 49, 57, 66, 77, 80, 86, 108, 117

myth, 5, 53, 86, 109, 111, 113-9, 133, 164-5

na gCopaleen, Myles, 15, 117

narrative, 5, 7, 48, 71, 101, 106-7,
111-2, 119-20, 123, 131-2, 144,
153, 157
national revival, 2, 4, 16, 18-9, 27, 41,
61, 105, 112, 132, 154
national theatre, 1, 4-5, 8, 11-2, 17,
19, 21, 23, 26-7, 31-7, 43, 47, 49,
53, 62, 65, 71, 73-4, 81, 86, 101,
132
nationalism, 4-5, 12-3, 16-7, 20-2, 25,
28, 30-2, 37, 42-3, 45-6, 52, 62,
65-6, 73, 75-6, 82, 85-6, 93, 95,
97, 99, 101, 111, 117, 119-20,
132, 142, 146-7, 149, 167
naturalism, 5, 49, 63, 72, 154, 160
nic Shiublaigh, Maire, 47
Northern Ireland, 1, 5, 6, 15, 105,
108, 110, 112, 131-3, 135-6, 140-
2, 144
O'Brien, Flann, 15, 117, 142; The
Third Policeman, 143; The Poor
Mouth (An Beál Bocht), 15, 117
O'Casey, Sean, 2, 5, 26, 71, 74-6, 80-
1, 90, 101-1; Cock-a-doodle
Dandy, 77; Juno and the Paycock,
74, 77; The Plough and the Stars,
26, 74-6; The Shadow of the
Gunman, 74; The Silver Tassie, 3,
5, 71, 77-8, 80-3, 85, 101-2
O'Donnell, F. Hugh, 27
O'Flaherty, Liam, 75, 90
O'Leary, John, 47
Orangeism, 147
Orton, Joe, 157
Owen, Wilfred, 82
Palo Alto psychology and
psychiatry, 121, 122, 123
paradox, 3, 20, 23, 35, 65, 111, 123-4,
139, 143, 152, 168
Parker, Stewart, 2, 5-6, 8, 50, 135-
50, 152-3; Heavenly Bodies, 142,
147, 149; The Iceberg, 141;
Northern Star, 142, 144-9;
Pentecost, 136, 140, 142, 147,

150-3; Pratt's Fall, 142;
Spokesong, 140-4, 146, 152
Parnell, Charles Stuart, 59, 91
parody, 40, 78, 85, 89-90, 96, 129,
147-8, 158, 165
pastiche, 90, 142, 144, 156
pastoral, 14, 57, 100-1, 164
Patterson, Johnny, 147-9
Paulin, Tom, 45, 105
Pearse, Padraic H., 32, 61, 64, 75,
91, 141
performativity, 99-100
Pethica, James, 15, 45, 46, 50
Pilkington, Lionel, 20, 25, 26, 29,
30, 32, 33, 34, 45, 48, 62, 73, 74,
77, 85, 102, 115-6
Pilling, John, 56
Pinter, Harold, 157
post-colonial theory, 2, 5, 66, 106-7,
111, 132, 169
postmodernism, 91, 156
post-structuralist theory, 3, 6
Price, Alan, 60, 63
Procházka, Martin, 4
provincialism, 43, 52, 58, 110, 135
puppets, 163, 168
Rea, Stephen, 105, 153
realism, 18, 20, 37, 40, 44, 49, 74, 78-
9, 83, 109, 150, 153, 166
Renan, Ernest, 16, 19
Republicanism, 76, 85, 91, 98, 111
Richards, Shaun, 132
Richtarik, Marilynn J., 106, 143,
144, 145, 146, 151
ritual, 17, 78, 122, 124, 128-30, 152
Robinson, Lennox, 73, 80
Roche, Anthony, 42, 57
Romanticism, 3-4, 6, 19, 57, 85,
138-9, 152, 168
Rudkin, David, 132; The Saxon
Shore, 132
Saddlemyer, Ann, 37, 41, 43, 45,
54, 64, 72
Sassoon, Siegfried, 82
Satake, Akiko, 145, 147

satire, 4, 6, 15, 40, 51-2, 63-5, 73, 77, 82, 90, 95-7, 101, 117, 158, 165-7
Schlegel, Friedrich, 3, 138-9, 152
Schnell, Ralf, 139
Shakespeare, William, 22, 148; *Hamlet*, 148; *Macbeth*, 108
Shan Van Vocht, 31, 45-6, 86, 95
Shaw, G.B., 73, 80, 91; *The Shewing-up of Blanco Posnet*, 73; *John Bull's Other Island*, 73; *O'Flaherty, V.C.*, 73
Sheehy-Skeffington, Hanna, 75
Shepard, Sam, 157; *True West*, 157
Sierz, Aleks, 156
sitcom, 154, 157
socialism, 77, 135
Spacks, Patricia Meyer, 60
St. Peter, Christine, 87, 90, 99
Stage Irishman, 13, 22
Steiner, George, 116-7
stereotypes, 35, 74, 102, 109-10, 115, 140, 156, 158, 164-5
Stork, Uwe, 40
Strindberg, August, 73
Synge, John Millington, 3-4, 6, 15, 18-9, 24-5, 35-67, 72-5, 83, 89-90, 97, 157, 167-8; *The Playboy of the Western World*, 24, 26, 30, 36, 39, 40-1, 43-4, 50-1, 59-66, 73, 75, 155, 157, 167; *Riders to the Sea*, 37, 42-6, 157; *(In) the Shadow of the Glen*, 19, 36, 37, 41, 43, 47-9, 51, 54, 58, 63; *The Well of the Saints*, 8, 40, 42-3, 51-4, 57, 90
Tarantino, Quentin, 158; *Reservoir Dogs*, 158
The Aeneid, 118
The Field Day Anthology, 106, 111, 132-3
The Man of Aran, 157, 166
Toller, Ernst, 87, 102

transcendence, 138, 140, 144, 152
translation, 15, 38-40, 52, 122, 132, 139
Tuohy, Patrick, 90
Ulster Cycle, 15
uncanny, 149, 161-2
Unionism, 132, 145-6
United Irishmen, 144-6
utopia, 5, 93, 97, 99, 133, 139
vampires, 33, 95, 145, 147
violence, 5, 63-5, 75, 100-1, 115, 124, 135, 140, 150, 155-6, 159-60, 162, 165, 167
Wagner, Richard, 30
Wallace, Clare, 156, 157, 158
War of Independence, 75
Waters, John, 155-6, 164, 165
Watson, G.J., 21
West of Ireland, 15, 24, 26, 36, 38, 40-1, 50, 59, 64, 66, 157, 167
Wilde, Oscar, 142
Woman of Ireland, 96-7, 145
Wordsworth, William, 19-20
World War I, 78, 80-2
Worth, Katharine, 38, 42
Wyndham, George, 47
Yeats, John Butler, 21
Yeats, William Butler, 1, 4, 8, 11-35, 36, 38-9, 42-3, 45-6, 48, 53, 55, 57, 62-3, 66, 72-5, 78, 80-3, 85, 86, 89, 91, 95, 97, 101-2, 116, 137
Cathleen ni Houlihan, 27, 31, 33-4, 45-6, 50, 85-6, 95, 97, 116, 145, 147; *The Countess Cathleen*, 18, 24, 27-30, 32, 34, 47, 65; *The Hour-Glass*, 24; *The King's Threshold*, 24; *The Land of Heart's Desire*, 14; *On Baile's Strand*, 89